CONTENTS

The aims of this block are:

1 To revise and extend those frequency domain modelling techniques most appropriate to digital signals and telecommunications systems.
2 To introduce some aspects of digital signal transmission.
3 To present sampling, quantisation and pulse code modulation (PCM).
4 To describe time division multiplexing (TDM) and the CCITT TDM hierarchy for PCM signals.

OBJECTIVES

Ideally, after studying this material you should be able to apply it appropriately in unfamiliar circumstances. The following specific objectives are an indication of the level of knowledge, skills and understanding you should have. You should refer to the *Course Guide* for details of the course team's view of Aims and Objectives.

Specific objectives

Objectives	Content area
Section 2: Systems and signals	
Use normalised frequency response curves to estimate amplitude ratio and phase shift. (SAQ 2.1)	frequency response
Sketch the line spectrum of a given square wave, or the waveform given the line spectrum. (SAQs 2.2, 2.5)	Fourier analysis
Relate time domain and frequency domain models of simple periodic signals. (SAQ 2.3)	
Relate channel bandwidth to signalling rate in baud or data rate in bits s^{-1}. (SAQ 2.4)	signalling over a bandlimited channel
Sketch simple bilateral spectra. (SAQ 2.6)	bilateral spectra
Explain the meaning of amplitude distortion and phase distortion and describe their effects.	amplitude distortion and phase distortion
Section 3: Modelling individual pulses	
Sketch the spectra of rectangular, triangular, and raised cosine pulses. (SAQs 3.1, 3.2, 3.3)	pulse spectra
Define what is meant by a linear system, and explain why linear models are useful in telecommunications.	linear systems
Explain how the input spectrum, output spectrum, and frequency response of a linear system are related.	
Relate general time domain pulse characteristics to corresponding frequency domain features and vice versa. (SAQ 3.4)	transform pairs
Section 4: Digital signal transmission	
Describe what is meant by ISI, and how an eye diagram can be used to estimate its effects.	intersymbol interference (ISI)
Explain why the raised cosine spectrum is a desirable goal for minimising ISI.	pulse shaping
Relate maximum signalling rate to channel bandwidth for a system using raised cosine shaping.	

Technology: A Third Level Course

T322
Digital Telecommunications

BLOCK 4 DIGITAL SIGNALS

Prepared for the Course Team by Chris Bissell

The Open University

The Course Team

Gaby Smol	(*Chairman*)
Jill Alger	(*Editor*)
Carolyn Baxter	(*Course manager*)
Chris Bissell	(*Electronics*)
David Chapman	(*Electronics*)
John Dillow	(*Consultant*)
Lem Ibbotson	(*Electronics*)
Michael Lewsey	(*Course manager*)
Adrian Rawlings	(*Electronics*)
David Reed	(*Electronics*)
John Taylor	(*Graphic artist*)
Rob Williams	(*Designer*)

External assessor
Professor B. G. Evans

The Open University
Walton Hall, Milton Keynes MK7 6AA

First published 1989 as part of PT629. Revised edition 1990. Reprinted 1997.
Reprinted with corrections 1993

Designed by the Graphic Design Group of the Open University.

Typeset in Great Britain by Alden Press Ltd, Northampton.

Printed in Great Britain by Henry Ling Ltd, The Dorset Press, Dorchester, Dorset DT1 1HD.

ISBN 0 7492 6046 7

1.3

Explain the need for line codes, and describe the desirable properties of alternate mark inversion (AMI) and HDB3 in this respect. (SAQs 4.1, 4.2)

line codes

Section 5: Pulse code modulation

State the sampling theorem for baseband signals.

sampling

Sketch the spectrum of a sampled signal, given the message spectrum and sampling rate. (SAQ 5.1)

Explain how a pulse amplitude modulated (PAM) waveform can be used to model a sampled signal.

Describe uniform and non-uniform encoding, and explain why the latter is used for voice telephony.

encoding and decoding

Estimate the bandwidth requirements of a single PCM speech channel. (SAQ 5.2)

PCM bandwidth requirements

State reasons why PCM is a desirable way of transmitting speech signals.

Describe how a message signal can be recovered from an ideal PCM signal.

signal recovery

Explain why using a sample and hold for signal recovery introduces amplitude distortion, and estimate the magnitude of such distortion. (SAQ 5.3)

Section 6: Systems aspects of pulse code modulation

Describe the principle of TDM and explain why it is used.

time division multiplexing

Outline the CCITT TDM hierarchy, and estimate the bandwidth requirements of the various levels.

Explain what is meant by the regeneration of a digital signal, and how it compares with the use of repeater amplifiers in analogue telephony.

regeneration

Sketch a functional block diagram of a typical codec, and explain the purpose of the various components. (SAQs 6.1, 6.2, 6.3)

codecs

Terminology

You should understand what is meant by the following terms:

aliasing
alternate mark inversion (AMI)
amplitude distortion
amplitude spectrum
anti-aliasing filter

baseband
baud

clock extraction
codec
companding
continuous spectrum
cosine series

data rate
dc term
dibit
double-sided spectrum

equaliser
even signal
eye diagram

Fourier analysis
Fourier series

Fourier transform pair
frame
frequency domain
frequency response
frequency spectrum

HDB3

intersymbol interference (ISI)

jitter

linear model
linear phase
line code
line spectrum
loss equalisation

negative frequency
non-linear encoding
non-uniform encoding
normalisation

phase distortion
primary level TDM
pulse amplitude modulation (PAM)
pulse code modulation (PCM)

quantisation distortion
quantisation level
quantisation noise

raised cosine spectrum
regeneration
regenerative repeater

sampling frequency
sampling rate
signalling rate
signal to quantisation-noise ratio
$(\sin x)/x$ function
single-sided spectrum
spectral density
spectrum

TDM hierarchy
threshold detector
time division multiplexing (TDM)
time domain
timing extraction

1 INTRODUCTION

In this block I shall consider in detail the physical and mathematical properties of the signals used in digital telecommunication systems.

The *Introduction* to T322 *Digital Telecommunications* described some of the properties of digital signals and considered why transmission using such signals is so attractive. To analyse the properties of digital signals in detail, however, requires a mathematical framework, and it is this framework which we turn to now. Many of the mathematical techniques used in telecommunications involve frequency domain models, in which signals are characterised by their spectra, and systems by their frequency response functions. You should have met these basic ideas before, but Sections 2 and 3 develop them in depth. These sections are fundamental to the whole of the course, and form the core of this block.

Later sections are concerned, in one way or another, with the application of the fundamental material of Sections 2 and 3. Section 4 applies frequency domain ideas to some of the problems of transmitting digital signals, while Section 5 examines how telephone speech signals (or, indeed, any other analogue signal) can be transmitted digitally. Section 6 concludes the block with a brief look at some elementary systems aspects of the public digital transmission network.

Like other blocks, *Digital Signals* includes both self-assessment questions (SAQs) and in-text questions. I cannot over-emphasise the importance of attempting these conscientiously. **Try each in-text question before reading on to the solution**. The questions are there for a purpose: to make you think about what has just gone before (or what is coming next) and to involve you more actively in your study. **Similarly, write out a full answer to each SAQ**. It will take longer than just making notes or simply 'thinking it through' but you will also learn a lot more.

2 SYSTEMS AND SIGNALS

Mathematical models of signals and systems are vital if we are to design new systems which will behave as required or analyse the behaviour of existing systems. As a starting point, let us briefly consider some of the effects that occur in a simple digital transmission system and which it is important to be able to analyse.

Figure 2.1 shows part of a system for transmitting binary data coded simply as two different voltage levels. I have assumed that the higher level corresponds to 1 and the lower to 0, although it is immaterial whether positive or negative logic is used. The transmission medium is simply a coaxial cable. Such systems are often used for interconnecting individual computers in local area networks, with coaxial links up to a few kilometres in length.

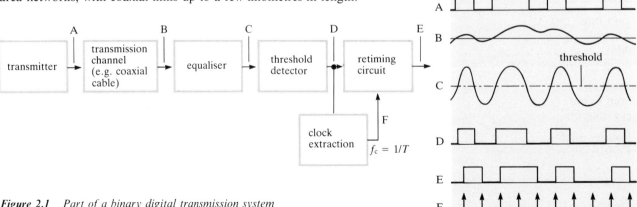

Figure 2.1   Part of a binary digital transmission system

Signals cannot be transmitted completely unchanged through any communication channel: there will always be effects which modify the waveform. Waveform B in Figure 2.1 illustrates (not to scale) possible distortion of the original binary signal after transmission via coaxial cable. The system is unable to respond immediately to sudden transitions in voltage level. In the received signal, therefore, the sharp distinction between the two signalling states, and hence between binary 1 and 0, has disappeared. There has also been considerable attenuation, the magnitude of which depends on the length of the cable. Note that in practice there is also a delay, again depending on the length of the cable. This is not shown explicitly; instead the waveforms are drawn as if the signal appeared instantaneously at the receiver, although in distorted form.

To counteract the effects illustrated, the receiver includes a circuit known as an *equaliser*, which partially compensates for the distortion introduced by the transmission channel. At the output of the equaliser waveform C has been 'sharpened' so that, although it is still far from being an accurate replica of the original binary waveform, which parts of the signal correspond to an original binary 0 and which to a 1 are now much clearer. Note that I have made one other important assumption when drawing these waveforms (apart from not indicating the delay), namely, that there is no noise to corrupt the signals.

equaliser

Waveform C, however, is still not in an appropriate form for input to a computer terminal as a binary waveform, or for retransmission through the network to other receivers. It first has to be sharpened even further to regenerate the original binary signal. To do this a *threshold detector* is used. The threshold detector gives an output which is always one of two values, depending whether the input signal is above or below a threshold level. After passing through the threshold detector, the signal waveform can be represented by D. It is very similar to the original binary signal except that the transitions from one level to the other are no longer perfectly in step with the original transitions.

threshold detector

☐ Why should there be such irregularities?

■ There is no reason to expect waveform C to cross the threshold at exactly the same instants of time as the original binary signal changed state. Distortion in the channel, the effects of the equaliser, as well as any noise, can all affect the exact timing of the threshold crossings and hence the transitions of waveform D.

The final stage shown in Figure 2.1 is therefore to retime the waveform so that the transitions take place at regularly spaced intervals, as illustrated by waveforms E and F. F represents the regular pulses of a clock signal used to provide the time reference. In a synchronous system the clock pulses are derived from the incoming signal. In the absence of noise, and with perfect retiming, waveform E would be a perfect replica of the original binary waveform. If you compare waveforms C and E you can see the combined effect of threshold detection and retiming. It is equivalent to determining the binary states of the distorted, equalised signal by sampling its value near its peaks and troughs. This is an important point, since timing the threshold decisions in this way will minimise the probability of error when the received signal is corrupted by noise.

Effects similar to those illustrated in Figure 2.1 are found in other digital telecommunication systems, and it is worth spending a few moments looking at one other example. Figure 2.2 represents the comparable effects in one type of optical fibre transmission system for telephone signals (again not to scale).

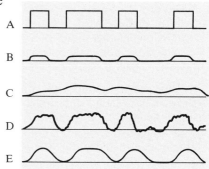

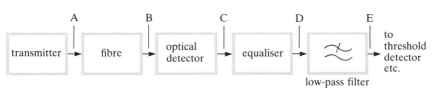

Figure 2.2 *Part of an optical fibre transmission system*

Here the original signals, from whatever source, are coded in binary form and are used to turn a laser on and off at high speed as the two signalling states. Transmission via optical fibre, as with any other medium, introduces distortion but in the case illustrated the major effect is severe attenuation: the transitions from one intensity level to another are still comparatively sharp (waveform B). Waveform C, however, illustrates the situation after the received light intensity has been converted into an electric current. Before this waveform can be applied to a threshold detector it must be equalised and low-pass filtered to remove high-frequency noise introduced by the receiver and equaliser. The important point is that here the equaliser compensates for *receiver* effects, rather than channel effects.

In both the cases shown in Figure 2.1 and Figure 2.2, the overall transmission process introduces distortion. To design systems to overcome such degradation, models of both signals and transmission channels are required. The types of model commonly used in telecommunications will form the subject matter of this section and the next. In most of the discussion I shall not consider the effects of noise, although this important topic will be taken up later in the course.

2.1 Linear models

A particularly important type of mathematical model used in many branches of science and technology is the *linear model*. The term requires some explanation, since it is only indirectly related to the word linear in the more usual sense of a straight line.

There are a number of equivalent definitions of linearity, but here I shall be concerned with only two of them. I shall state them first, since you are probably familiar with at least one definition, and then explain why they are so important.

1　A linear system is one which obeys the principle of superposition. That is, if an input $x_1(t)$ to the system produces an output $y_1(t)$, and an input $x_2(t)$ produces an output $y_2(t)$, then an input $x_1(t) + x_2(t)$ produces an output $y_1(t) + y_2(t)$.

2　A linear system is one possessing the 'frequency preservation' property. That is, the steady state response of a linear system to a sinusoidal input is itself sinusoidal, having the same frequency as the input but generally differing in amplitude and phase.

To see why the concept of linearity in this more general sense is so important, look again at Figure 2.1 and consider how the effects of transmission of the binary input signal might be calculated. We need some model of the behaviour of the various system elements in order to do this. For example, let us suppose for simplicity that waveform A is processed by a system element which can be modelled as a first-order low-pass filter of the type you should be familiar with from your previous experience. In this case the response of the system element to an isolated rectangular pulse is as shown in Figure 2.3.

The principle of superposition means that, if the system element behaves in a reasonably linear way, its overall response to a complicated binary waveform made up of a number of rectangular pulses can be calculated by adding together the responses to the individual pulses. For example, the response of a first-order low-pass filter to the binary waveform A of Figure 2.4 is as waveform B. Exactly the same principle applies to a complete linear transmission channel rather than just to a single component. Figure 2.5(a) illustrates a possible pulse response of a channel and Figure 2.5(b) shows the cumulative effect of such a channel on a segment of a digital signal.

This 'superposition' approach is an extremely useful way of analysing the behaviour of a digital transmission system, and will be discussed in more detail in Section 4. Note that it is particularly convenient because digital signals are constructed from a limited range of basic signal shapes. In the examples considered so far, the digital waveforms can be viewed as a sequence of rectangular pulses, each with a similar pulse response waveform.

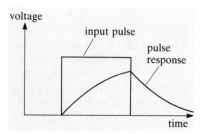

Figure 2.3 Rectangular pulse response of a first-order low-pass filter where the time constant and pulse duration are similar

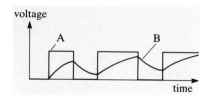

Figure 2.4 Response of a first-order low-pass filter to a binary waveform

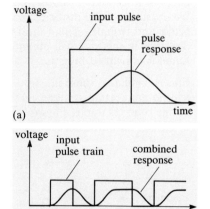

Figure 2.5 Response of a telecommunication channel to (a) a rectangular pulse and (b) a binary waveform

An alternative approach to modelling the behaviour of a transmission channel is based on the second definition of linearity given above. As will be discussed in more detail below, any practical message signal can be described in terms of its frequency content or, to be more precise, modelled as an appropriate *frequency spectrum*. Similarly, any linear system can be completely specified by its *frequency response*, that is, a description of the amplitude changes and phase shifts introduced for all frequencies. (Remember, a linear system in the steady state modifies each input sinusoid to give an output sinusoid of the same frequency, but generally differing in amplitude and phase.) So the spectrum of a signal tells us what frequencies are present in a signal, while the system frequency response tells us how each of these frequencies is 'processed' by the linear system. Given the spectrum of the input and the frequency response of the system, it is often possible to calculate the spectrum of the output without difficulty. Modelling signals and systems in such *frequency domain* terms is a useful – and completely equivalent – alternative to *time domain* modelling using pulse responses. A constant theme of this block will be the need to 'switch' between time domain and frequency domain models as appropriate.

frequency spectrum
frequency response

frequency domain
time domain
The 'input–output' approach in the frequency domain will be developed later.

Figure 2.6 shows the frequency response of a first-order low-pass filter. Such a frequency response might model a simple *RC* network or a more complicated system component such as an amplifier. Note that a logarithmic scale is used for the frequency axis, and that it is labelled in multiples of the cut-off frequency f_c of the first-order filter. The amplitude ratio is expressed in decibels, that is:

$$\text{amplitude ratio in dB} = 20 \log \frac{\text{output amplitude}}{\text{input amplitude}}$$

and a dc or low-frequency gain of 1 (0 dB) is assumed. If the dc gain is other than unity the whole plot can be scaled accordingly. For an amplitude ratio expressed in dB this scaling corresponds to shifting the whole curve up or down as appropriate.

Figure 2.6 Normalised frequency response of a first-order low-pass filter

amplitude ratio/dB

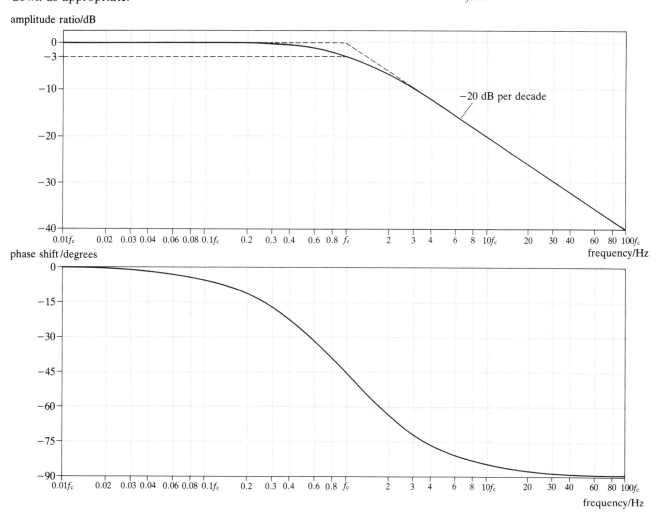

phase shift /degrees

In the form of Figure 2.6 the amplitude ratio is said to be normalised with respect to the dc gain, while the frequency is normalised with respect to the cut-off frequency. Such *normalisation* means that a single frequency response plot can be used for systems with *any* values of dc gain or cut-off frequency, simply by appropriate scaling.

normalisation

Both the amplitude ratio and phase shift of a first-order low-pass filter can be expressed as the single mathematical function

$$H(f) = \frac{k}{1 + jf/f_c}$$

where k is the low frequency or dc gain, f_c is the cut-off frequency and $j^2 = -1$. In general $H(f)$ takes on a complex value for any given value of frequency f and defines the steady-state sinusoidal response. At any frequency f, the amplitude ratio is given by $|H(f)|$ and the phase shift $\theta(f) = \angle H(f)$, using the normal rules of complex numbers. Figure 2.6 was plotted in this way, and similar frequency response functions can be derived for more complicated systems. You do not need to be skilled in using such expressions for this course, but you should have met them before.

To check that you know how to use frequency response functions in the form of normalised curves, try the following revision SAQ.

> **SAQ 2.1 (Revision)**   A system is modelled as a first-order low-pass filter with unity dc gain and a cut-off frequency of 4 kHz. A sinusoidal voltage with an amplitude of 10 V and a frequency of 8 kHz is applied to the system input. What is the amplitude of the output signal in the steady state, and what is its phase shift with respect to the input signal?

A frequency response model of a telecommunications channel (or indeed many other types of system) is an extremely useful tool. As illustrated by SAQ 2.1, quantitative results relating to individual sinusoids can be obtained very easily. Even more importantly, however, if the general frequency domain characteristics of an input signal are known – such as the range of frequencies likely to be present – a frequency response model can give an immediate 'feel' for how the channel will behave in general terms, without the need for complex calculation. There is only one problem: how can a digital message signal such as those illustrated in Figures 2.1 or 2.2 be categorised in terms of a 'range of frequencies likely to be present'? Section 2.2 deals with this problem.

2.2 Fourier analysis

The material in this subsection may be familiar to you. Nevertheless, you should study it carefully, trying the ITQs and SAQs as revision exercises.

In 1822 Jean Baptiste Joseph Fourier introduced a technique which has proved to have far-reaching consequences for many branches of technology. One way of stating Fourier's classic result is as follows:

Any periodic signal $f(t)$ can be expressed as a series, possibly infinite, of sinusoidal components, such that

$$f(t) = A_0 + A_1 \cos(\omega t + \phi_1) + A_2 \cos(2\omega t + \phi_2)$$

$$+ A_3 \cos(3\omega t + \phi_3) + \ldots$$

where the fundamental angular frequency ω of the *Fourier series* is related to the repetition period T_p of the signal $f(t)$ by the expression $\omega = 2\pi/T_p$, and the Fourier coefficients $A_1, A_2, A_3 \ldots$ and $\phi_1, \phi_2, \phi_3 \ldots$ are constants.

The particular way I have chosen to present this result is called a Fourier *cosine series*. The series may equally well be expressed as a sum of sine functions, however, or as a mixture of sine and cosine terms. I find the cosine series the easiest approach to the theoretical development of this subsection.

The coefficients A_1, A_2, A_3, etc. represent the amplitudes of the sinusoidal

In this block I shall use both hertz (Hz) and radians per second (rad s^{-1}) as units of frequency, depending on which is more appropriate to the particular circumstances. You will find both rad s^{-1} and Hz used in the published literature on telecommunications, so it is as well to become familiar with both. It is also sensible when attempting numerical exercises to note *before starting work* which units are used!

Fourier series

cosine series

components, while ϕ_1, ϕ_2, ϕ_3, etc. represent their phase angles. (By a sinusoid I mean any signal of the form $A \sin(\omega t + \phi)$ or $B \cos(\omega t + \theta)$.)

There are standard mathematical expressions for deriving the values of the amplitude and phase coefficients from the particular signal $f(t)$. You do not need to know them for this course, but if you are interested in studying the topic further, the course T326 *Electronic Signal Processing* (Open University, 1984) covers the subject in detail. Other texts suitable for background or further reading are listed at the end of this block.

What the above theorem means is that for modelling purposes any periodic signal can be treated exactly as if it consisted of a number of individual sinusoids. Such *Fourier analysis* of a periodic signal into its Fourier components gives us the frequency spectrum model referred to earlier. For example, suppose that we wish to transmit the periodic binary signal

$$\ldots 10101010 \ldots$$

using $+V$ and $-V$ to represent the two binary states, as in the link between a terminal and a modem. The transmitted waveform would therefore approximate to Figure 2.7. (The waveform is drawn symmetrically about the time origin simply for mathematical convenience.)

Fourier analysis

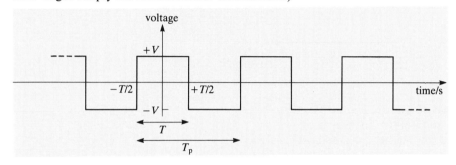

The Fourier series representing the waveform of Figure 2.7 can be calculated using standard mathematical results. It is

$$f(t) = \frac{4V}{\pi}\left[\cos \omega t + \tfrac{1}{3}\cos(3\omega t + \pi) + \tfrac{1}{5}\cos 5\omega t\right.$$
$$\left. + \tfrac{1}{7}\cos(7\omega t + \pi) + \cdots\right]$$

where again $\omega = 2\pi/T_\mathrm{p}$. The repetition period is twice the duration of a single signalling element, T, so we can write $T_\mathrm{p} = 2T$.

Note that only odd harmonics, that is, only odd multiples of ω, are present in the series. Fourier components therefore occur only at odd multiples of $2\pi/T_\mathrm{p}\ \mathrm{rad\,s^{-1}}$, that is, at odd multiples of $1/T_\mathrm{p}$ Hz. Note also that there is no dc term ($A_0 = 0$). The phase angles of the harmonics are alternately 0 and π rad.

    ☐ Why is there no dc term?

    ■ The dc term represents the average value of the signal $f(t)$. As Figure 2.7 clearly shows, the average value in this case is zero.

The Fourier series corresponding to the binary signal of Figure 2.7 can be represented as a *line spectrum*, a diagram showing the amplitudes of the frequencies present in the series together with their phase relationships. In general it is most convenient to draw separate amplitude and phase spectra, as in Figure 2.8. The frequency axis is labelled in hertz in order to bring out the relationship between the duration of a signalling element, T, and features of the spectrum.

I have already remarked that the phase angles of the components of this particular signal are either 0 or π rad (0 or 180°). This is an example of a general feature of all signals whose graphs are symmetric under reflection about the vertical (voltage) axis. Figure 2.7 shows that this is the case here: formally we can write $f(t) = f(-t)$. Such waveforms are known as *even*, and the cosine series components of *even signals* all have phase angles of 0 or $\pm\pi$ rad. I mention this because it brings about a simplification in the

Any real signal has to be switched on at some moment in time. We assume in cases like Figure 2.7 that the signal has existed in its periodic form for a sufficiently long period of time to stabilise before we take an interest in it.

Figure 2.7 A square wave representing the binary sequence ...10101010...

line spectrum

even signal

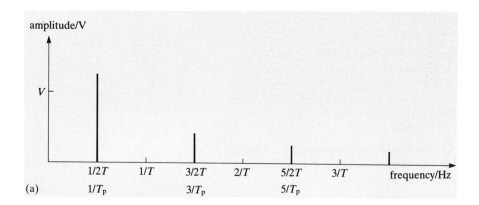

(a)

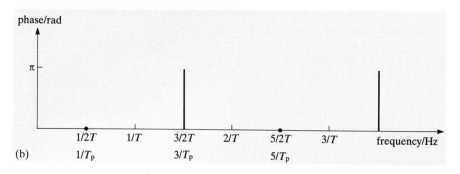

(b)

Figure 2.8 Line spectrum of the square wave of Figure 2.7 as separate amplitude and phase spectra

spectral representation. A phase angle of $\pm\pi$ rad ($\pm180°$) can be thought of as equivalent to multiplication of the Fourier coefficient by -1: $\cos(\omega t \pm \pi)$ can be written as $-\cos\omega t$. Hence, for even signals, a single spectral diagram can represent both amplitude and phase spectra. This is illustrated for the ...10101010... waveform in Figure 2.9, where antiphase components are represented by negative lines. In the general case, however, amplitude and phase terms need to be specified separately.

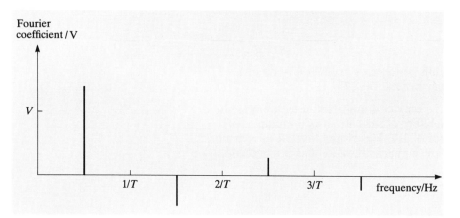

Figure 2.9 An alternative representation of the line spectrum of Figure 2.8

SAQ 2.2 Draw a line spectrum similar to Figure 2.9 to represent the periodic binary signal

...0011001100110011...

Label the frequency axis in terms of T, the duration of one signalling element.

The binary signal of alternating states represented in Figure 2.7 is a useful 'worst-case' waveform for evaluating certain aspects of telecommunication system performance. Because such a signal represents the fastest rate of switching between the two possible signalling states, it also has the spectrum with the highest-frequency components. All telecommunication channels have an upper limit to the frequencies which can be transmitted effectively. The spectrum of the ...10101010... waveform of Figure 2.7 is therefore a useful measure of the worst-case bandwidth requirements of this particular system.

SAQ 2.3 A binary signal similar to that of Figure 2.7 is transmitted through a first-order low-pass filter. The duration of each signalling element (binary 1 or 0) is 10 ms. In the absence of noise, would you expect the output waveform to be a close replica of the input signal if the cut-off frequency of the channel is (a) 150 Hz; (b) 1.5 kHz? Justify your answer in each case.

Of course, in a digital system it is not necessary for the original waveform to be transmitted unchanged. What is vital, however, is for the distinction between transmitted binary 1 and 0 to be completely unambiguous at the receiver, whatever the particular pattern of 1s and 0s in the message happens to be.

☐ Suppose that the ... 10101010 ... binary signal is transmitted through an *ideal* low-pass channel which eliminates all but the first harmonic of the Fourier series, and passes the first harmonic unchanged. Would it be possible to distinguish between the two signalling states at the receiver? If the data rate is 100 bits s^{-1}, what is the minimum bandwidth required to transmit this first harmonic?

■ Figure 2.10 illustrates the transmitted and received waveforms, assuming no time delay in the channel. Although the individual pulses are no longer rectangular, it is clear which parts of the received waveform represent a transmitted 1 and which a 0. For a data rate of 100 bits s^{-1} the duration of each signalling element is 10 ms as in SAQ 2.3. The frequency of the first harmonic, as found in SAQ 2.3, is $1/(2 \times 10^{-2})$ Hz or 50 Hz, so this is the required bandwidth.

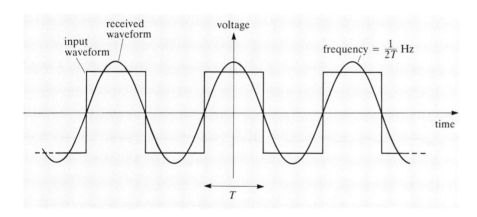

Figure 2.10 *A square wave and its fundamental Fourier component*

In fact this result is an illustration of an important theoretical limit to the maximum rate of signalling over a given bandlimited channel or, to put it the other way round, the minimum bandwidth required for a given rate of signalling. For the types of binary signal I have been considering so far, the channel must be able to pass very low frequencies, since a long string consisting entirely of binary 1s or entirely of 0s will represent a constant voltage level for a certain length of time. The channel bandwidth must also be at least wide enough to pass the first harmonic of the 'fastest changing' digital signal. For a simple binary signal, as you have already seen, the fastest changing signal is a stream of alternating 1s and 0s and the frequency of this first harmonic is $1/2T$ Hz where T is the duration of one signalling element in seconds. To transmit a binary signal at a rate of $1/T$ bits s^{-1} therefore requires a channel bandwidth of at least $1/2T$ Hz. Conversely, the maximum rate of binary signalling over a bandlimited channel of bandwidth B Hz is $2B$ bits s^{-1}.

For a non-binary digital signal, the fastest changing signal is one corresponding to the alternation between any two signalling states. Figure 2.11 illustrates this in the context of a signal using three different voltage levels for its three signalling states. In each case the figure includes the fundamental harmonic of the Fourier series representing the digital waveform: in the absence of noise the original digital signal could be reconstructed by accurately sampling this fundamental. (Note that the frequency of the fundamental of waveform (a) is identical to that of

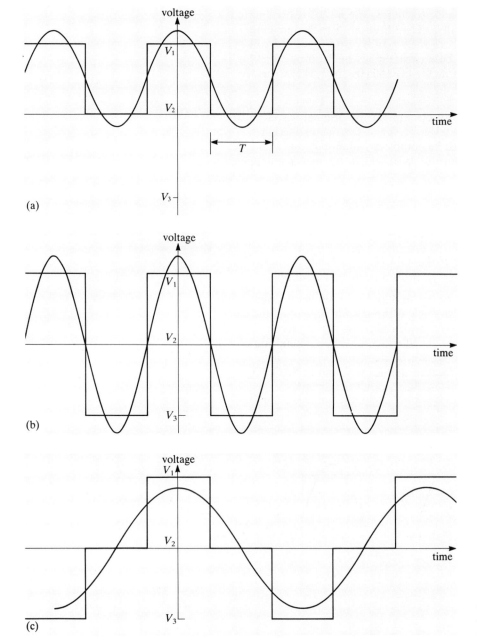

(a)

(b)

(c)

Figure 2.11 *Three ternary waveforms and their fundamental Fourier components. Waveforms (a) and (b) alternate between two signalling states, while (c) involves all three states*

waveform (b).) The frequency of the fundamental again corresponds to the absolute minimum bandwidth required to transmit the digital information. The two examples of alternation between two signalling states represent the 'worst case', with the highest-frequency fundamental. This frequency is therefore the minimum theoretical bandwidth required for information transmission. It is again $1/2T$ Hz for transmission at a rate of $1/T$ states s^{-1}. (As I shall discuss in a moment, however, $1/T$ states s^{-1} is *not* the same as $1/T$ bits s^{-1} where a non-binary signal is concerned.)

The preceding discussion is an illustration of a general rule:

The maximum theoretical signalling rate, S states s^{-1}, of a digital signal over an ideal bandlimited channel of bandwidth B Hz is given by the expression

$$S = 2 \times B$$

2.2.1 Signalling rate and data rate

For a binary signal, the above theoretical result means that the maximum data rate in bits s^{-1} is equal to twice the bandwidth. However, if a *non-binary* digital signal is involved, then the relationship between data rate and channel bandwidth is a little different. For example, in high-speed data transmission, 4, 8, 16, or even more distinct signalling states are often used,

I have not given a formal proof of this statement. My discussion simply presents supporting evidence in terms of the spectrum of the worst-case waveform. A rigorous proof requires a detailed mathematical treatment which would be out of place here.

This idea was first presented in the *Introduction*.

rather than only 2. In such systems each signalling state can be used to represent more than one bit of data. To illustrate this, consider a quaternary (4-state) system where the four states are simply called A, B, C and D. (The precise form these states take is not important here, but will be considered in a later block.) Each signalling state can be allocated to a particular combination of binary digits known as *dibits*:

dibits

Signalling state	Dibit
A	0 0
B	0 1
C	1 0
D	1 1

In systems like this it is useful to distinguish between the *data rate* in bits s^{-1} and the *signalling rate* (states s^{-1}) in *baud*.

data rate
signalling rate   *baud*

So, for example, in a quaternary transmission system such as that outlined above, a data rate of 2400 bits s^{-1} would correspond to a signalling rate of 1200 baud, since each signalling state corresponds to two binary digits.

□   A digital microwave transmission system uses 8 different signalling states. What is the relationship between bits s^{-1} and baud for this system?

■   If 8 states are possible, each can be used to represent 3 bits: 000 to 111. The data rate in bits s^{-1} is therefore three times the signalling rate in baud.

The term 'baud' derives from J.M.E. Baudot, an early worker in digital telecommunications. You should be aware that the term 'baud' is sometimes used incorrectly, as a synonym for 'bits s^{-1}'. Be careful, therefore, if you come across transmission rates expressed in baud, or 'baud rates' in bits s^{-1} for non-binary signals.

I have so far considered only systems where the signalling states are different voltage levels, and where the message signal spectrum extends down to very low frequencies, requiring a low-pass transmission channel. Such signals are often known as *baseband* digital signals. The relationship between bandwidth and signalling rate is quite general, however, and applies to other digital transmission systems, for example, those involving modulated carriers, where the spectrum of the digital message signal does not extend to low frequencies. However, it should be emphasised that the limit is a theoretical one, and can only be approached, not achieved, in practice. The topic will be discussed in more detail in Section 4.

baseband

SAQ 2.4   What is the minimum theoretical bandwidth required to transmit data at a rate of 4800 bits s^{-1} using (a) binary and (b) quaternary transmission systems?

2.2.2   Signals with a dc component

The spectra considered so far have all lacked a dc component, as the corresponding time waveforms have all had zero average value. Many digital waveforms used in practice do possess a dc term, however, the magnitude of which is represented on a spectrum by a line at zero frequency.

SAQ 2.5   Quickly sketch the square wave, part of whose spectrum is shown in Figure 2.12. (Refer to Figures 2.7 and 2.9 if necessary.)

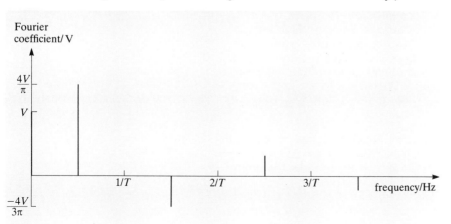

Figure 2.12   *Line spectrum for SAQ 2.5*

2.3 Bilateral spectra

A diagram like Figure 2.8 or 2.9 is not the only way of representing the spectrum of a periodic signal. A very common alternative method makes use of a mathematical relationship between the sine, cosine, and exponential functions, known as Euler's theorem.

Euler's theorem states that

$$\exp(j\theta) = \cos\theta + j\sin\theta$$

where θ can take on any value and $j^2 = -1$ as usual.

Similarly,

$$\exp(-j\theta) = \cos\theta - j\sin\theta$$

Adding these two expressions leads to the result

$$\exp(j\theta) + \exp(-j\theta) = 2\cos\theta$$

or

$$\cos\theta = \tfrac{1}{2}[\exp(j\theta) + \exp(-j\theta)]$$

Using this final expression any cosine term can be rewritten as the sum of two exponential terms. For example, if the cosine term represents a sinusoid of frequency ω rad s^{-1}, we have

$$\cos\omega t = \tfrac{1}{2}\exp(j\omega t) + \tfrac{1}{2}\exp(-j\omega t)$$

By extending our notion of the term 'spectrum', the exponential terms can also be represented on a spectral diagram, as shown in Figure 2.13. The *single-sided amplitude spectrum* representing cos ωt is shown in (a), and its corresponding exponential or *double-sided* form in (b). Because the exponential form contains two terms, one expressed in terms of ω and one in terms of $-\omega$, the frequency axis of the spectrum is extended to include so-called *negative frequencies*.

Do not try to imagine what a signal with a negative frequency might be like, however – the idea is meaningless! Any real sinusoid has a particular frequency expressed as a positive number. If we choose to express such a sinusoid as the combination of two exponential terms, we shall always find that one is a function of ω and one of $-\omega$. Taken together, these positive and negative terms are an equivalent mathematical representation of the sinusoid. Note that the amplitude of each exponential term is equal to half the amplitude of the original cosine term. In general, the cosine term

$$f(t) = A\cos\omega t$$

can be rewritten

$$f(t) = \frac{A}{2}\exp(j\omega t) + \frac{A}{2}\exp(-j\omega t)$$

   ↑   ↑

positive frequency   negative frequency
amplitude   amplitude

The notion of a double-sided spectrum, involving 'negative' frequencies, may seem at first sight to be an unnecessary complication. However, it is a representation which has a number of advantages. Some of these will become apparent shortly, and I shall point them out as they arise. Admittedly, the greatest advantages are in material more mathematical than you will find in this course, so they will not be exploited to the full here. Nevertheless, the notation is widely used in signal processing and telecommunications, and you will need to be able to handle it in order to understand more advanced texts.

The spectrum of Figure 2.13 was the simplest possible: a single cosine term with amplitude 1 and zero phase angle. Similar double-sided spectra can also be drawn for more complicated signals. To start with, consider the case of the signal

$$f(t) = \cos(\omega t + \phi)$$

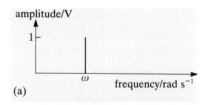

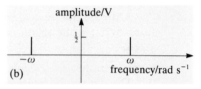

Figure 2.13 *Single-sided and double-sided spectrum of cos ωt*

single-sided amplitude spectrum
double-sided amplitude spectrum

negative frequencies

16

□ Write this in exponential form.

■ Using the expression derived earlier we have

$$\cos(\omega t + \phi) = \tfrac{1}{2}\exp[j(\omega t + \phi)] + \tfrac{1}{2}\exp[j(-\omega t - \phi)]$$

Using the normal rule for manipulating powers and exponents,
$\exp(a + b) = \exp(a)\exp(b)$

$$\cos(\omega t + \phi) = \tfrac{1}{2}\exp(j\omega t)\exp(j\phi) + \tfrac{1}{2}\exp(-j\omega t)\exp(-j\phi)$$

To show how this expression can be converted into a double-sided spectrum, I shall first rearrange it slightly:

$$\cos(\omega t + \phi) = \underbrace{\tfrac{1}{2}\exp(j\phi)}_{\substack{\text{positive frequency}\\\text{coefficient}}}\exp(j\omega t) + \underbrace{\tfrac{1}{2}\exp(-j\phi)}_{\substack{\text{negative frequency}\\\text{coefficient}}}\exp(-j\omega t)$$

I have identified 'coefficients' associated with each frequency term. Consider first the positive frequency coefficient, $\tfrac{1}{2}\exp(j\phi)$. This is a complex number written in polar form $r\exp(j\phi)$, where r is the magnitude (or amplitude) and ϕ the angle (or phase). So the complex coefficient includes both amplitude and phase information. Its amplitude is $\tfrac{1}{2}$ and its phase ϕ.

□ What are the amplitude and phase of the negative frequency term?

■ The amplitude of the negative component can be identified as $\tfrac{1}{2}$ (just as before); the phase this time is $-\phi$.

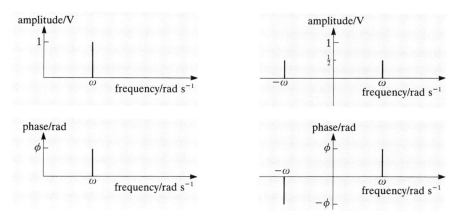

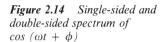

Armed with this information the double-sided spectrum of $\cos(\omega t + \phi)$ can be plotted as shown in Figure 2.14 (the single-sided spectrum is also shown for comparison). Note again that the amplitudes of both the positive and the negative frequency components are equal to half the amplitude of the single-sided spectral component. The double-sided phase spectrum, however, is rather different. The phase of the positive frequency term is identical to that of the original sinusoid $\cos(\omega t + \phi)$, while the phase of the negative frequency term is of the opposite sign. These amplitude and phase features are examples of a more general rule: the double-sided amplitude spectrum of any real signal is symmetric about $\omega = 0$, while the phase spectrum is antisymmetric. This is illustrated for a general line spectrum in Figure 2.15.

Figure 2.14 *Single-sided and double-sided spectrum of* $\cos(\omega t + \phi)$

SAQ 2.6
(a) Sketch the bilateral amplitude and phase line spectra of the signals represented by the expression

(i) $f(t) = 5\cos(\omega t + \pi/2)$

(ii) $f(t) = R\cos(\omega t - \alpha)$, where R and α are positive constants

(iii) $f(t) = \cos\omega t + \tfrac{1}{2}\cos(3\omega t + \pi/4)$

(b) Sketch the bilateral *amplitude* line spectra corresponding to (i) Figure 2.7 and (ii) Figure 2.12.

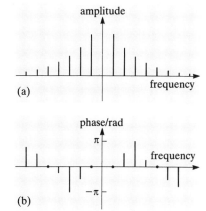

Figure 2.15 *A general line spectrum illustrating (a) the symmetric amplitude spectrum and (b) the antisymmetric phase spectrum*

2.4 Amplitude distortion and phase distortion

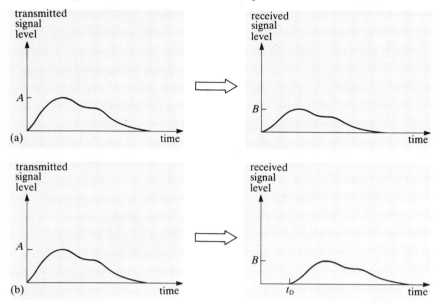

Figure 2.16 Transmitted and received signals for a distortionless channel: (a) with zero time delay; (b) with a constant transmission delay for all frequencies

An ideal transmission channel would pass all frequency components of a signal with their amplitude and phase relationships unchanged. Then the received signal would be a perfect (scaled) replica of the transmitted signal, as illustrated in Figure 2.16(a). The simplest frequency response model of such a distortionless channel would be a constant amplitude ratio and zero phase shift for all frequencies of interest. A zero phase shift for all frequencies, however, implies zero time delay, as assumed in Figure 2.16(a): a transmitted sinusoid of any frequency then would have to appear instantaneously at the receiver! The best we can hope for in practice (and even this is an unattainable ideal case) is that all sinusoidal components should be delayed by exactly the same length of time. Then the signal profile will still be undistorted (provided that the amplitude ratio is constant) but there will be a constant transmission delay t_D for all signals, as illustrated by Figure 2.16(b).

Such a constant time delay can be expressed easily as a phase characteristic. If all sinusoidal signals must be delayed by a time t_D, then a transmitted $A \sin \omega t$ will be received as $B \sin [\omega (t - t_D)]$, where B/A is the constant amplitude ratio defining the scaling referred to above. The received signal can be rewritten as

$$B \sin (\omega t - \omega t_D)$$

Comparing this with the general form $B \sin (\omega t + \theta)$ shows that the term $\theta = -\omega t_D$ can be interpreted as the phase characteristic illustrated in Figure 2.17, that is, a phase lag proportional to frequency. (Note that a linear frequency axis is used here in contrast to the logarithmic axis of Figure 2.6.) Such a characeristic is known as a *linear phase* characteristic.

A channel with an amplitude ratio which is not constant for all frequencies of interest is said to introduce *amplitude distortion*, while one whose phase characteristic is not linear introduces *phase distortion*.

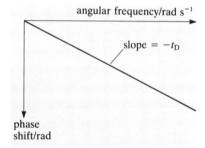

Figure 2.17 A linear phase characteristic corresponding to a transmission delay of t_D seconds

linear phase

amplitude distortion
phase distortion

☐ Does a first-order low-pass filter with a cut-off frequency of 4 kHz introduce amplitude distortion, phase distortion, or both over the frequency range 0 to 8 kHz?

■ Both. Clearly the amplitude ratio is not constant over this range, and Figure 2.6, although plotted on a logarithmic frequency axis, shows that the phase is non-linear. (For example, it tends towards a constant $-90°$ as the frequency is increased indefinitely.)

One important feature of linear phase is illustrated by Figure 2.18, which shows possible rectangular pulse responses of channels which introduce (a) both amplitude *and* phase distortion and (b) amplitude distortion alone.

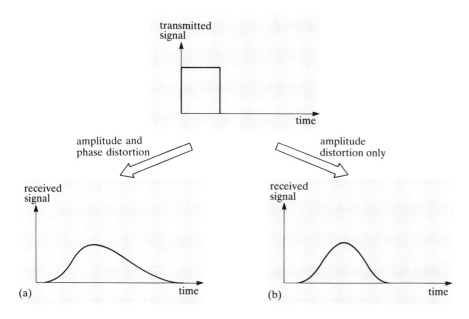

Figure 2.18 *Distortion of a rectangular pulse: (a) both amplitude and phase distortion; (b) amplitude distortion alone*

Note that in both cases the rectangular pulse shape transmitted has been distorted, but that the received pulse is asymmetric when both amplitude distortion and phase distortion occur, and symmetric when only amplitude distortion takes place. This is extremely significant for digital transmission, when symmetric pulses are transmitted in regular time slots. An overall linear phase characteristic means that the received pulses are also symmetric, and it is then easier to prevent pulses in one time slot 'spreading out' into adjacent ones. (This topic will be discussed in Section 4.2.) I shall assume in the remainder of this block that transmission channels have an overall linear phase characteristic, although it must be stressed here that a great deal of engineering effort is necessary to ensure a reasonably close approximation to this ideal. Discussion of how linear phase is approximated in practice is outside the scope of this course.

You may recall the asymmetric pulse response of a first-order low-pass filter illustrated in Figure 2.3 and the symmetric channel pulse response of Figure 2.5.

2.5 Summary

Any periodic signal can be modelled as a line spectrum specifying the amplitude and phase relationships of the individual Fourier components. Similarly, a linear telecommunications channel can be fully described by its frequency response, which specifies the steady-state amplitude ratio and phase shift at any given frequency.

Such frequency domain techniques are useful for both qualitative and quantitative interpretations of system behaviour. In particular, a consideration of the spectra of 'worst-case' digital signals leads to a fundamental relationship between maximum signalling rate and available bandwidth:

The maximum theoretical signalling rate, S states s^{-1}, over a bandlimited channel of bandwidth B Hz is given by the expression $S = 2 \times B$.

Double-sided or bilateral spectra are obtained by viewing a sinusoidal signal component as a pair of exponential components. This representation has various mathematical advantages over single-sided spectra, and is widely used in telecommunications and signal processing.

A channel whose amplitude ratio is constant over the frequency range of interest is said to introduce no amplitude distortion. Phase distortion occurs when the phase characteristic of a channel deviates from the ideal linear phase condition. The response of a channel with a linear phase characteristic to a transmitted rectangular pulse is a received pulse which, although distorted, is symmetric.

3 MODELLING INDIVIDUAL PULSES

Most message waveforms in digital systems are not periodic in nature, since it is the very unpredictability of the message which conveys the information. As has been seen already, however, certain periodic waveforms represent important limiting cases. In this section I want to examine another type of extreme case, and explain briefly how an *isolated* pulse can be represented by a spectrum, and why this particular special case is so important in digital telecommunications.

The general approach is to look at how the spectrum of a periodic pulse train changes as the individual pulses are separated by increasingly long intervals of time.

3.1 The spectrum of an isolated, rectangular pulse

As a starting point, consider the line spectrum of the periodic, rectangular pulse train shown in Figure 3.1. Unlike the waveform of Figure 2.7, the 'high' and 'low' voltages are not of equal duration: it is no longer a square wave. This makes the Fourier series a little more complicated, but standard Fourier analysis techniques lead to the Fourier cosine series:

$$f(t) = \frac{V\tau}{T} + \sum_{n=1}^{\infty} 2V\left[\frac{\sin(n\pi\tau/T)}{n\pi}\right]\cos n\omega t$$

where again $\omega = 2\pi/T$. I am now using T, not T_p, to represent the repetition period, and τ to represent the duration of one pulse. Note also that because T and ω are related to each other, there are various other ways of writing the Fourier series: I have chosen this particular form to bring out the important spectral characteristics.

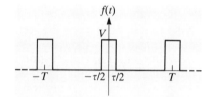

Figure 3.1 *A periodic, rectangular pulse train*

☐ Write out the first few terms of the series in full. Identify both the dc term and the Fourier coefficient of the fundamental component.

dc   Fourier coefficient
term   of fundamental

↓   ↓

$$\blacksquare \quad f(t) = \frac{V\tau}{T} + \overbrace{\frac{2V}{\pi}\sin\frac{\pi\tau}{T}}\cos\omega t + \frac{V}{\pi}\sin\frac{2\pi\tau}{T}\cos 2\omega t$$

$$+ \frac{2V}{3\pi}\sin\frac{3\pi\tau}{T}\cos 3\omega t$$

You do not need to remember this Fourier series, or know how it is derived. Check, however, that it is consistent with the spectra considered earlier of binary waveforms for which $\tau = T/2$.

The single-sided and double-sided line spectra corresponding to this series are shown in Figure 3.2 for the particular case of $\tau = T/4$. As before, the frequency axis is labelled in Hz rather than rad s^{-1}. The important points to remember about this figure are:

1 The spacing between the individual lines is $1/T$, the repetition frequency of the pulse train.

2 The dc term, representing the average value of $f(t)$, is equal to $V\tau/T$, in this case $V/4$.

3 The spectral lines can be viewed as possessing an 'envelope' which becomes zero for frequencies which are integral multiples of $1/\tau$, where τ is the pulse width.

4 The term $[\sin(n\pi\tau/T)]/n\pi$ in the Fourier series changes sign periodically as n varies. A negative term, and hence a corresponding negative Fourier coefficient, is interpreted as a phase angle of 180° for that particular sinusoidal component. Hence the phase of groups of components alternates, as indicated on the figure by groups of positive and negative lines in the way introduced in the previous section.

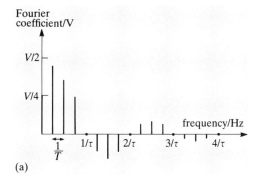

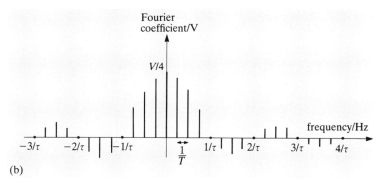

Figure 3.2 (a) Single-sided and (b) double-sided spectrum of the pulse train of Figure 3.1

From now on I shall deal only with double-sided spectra. Figure 3.3 illustrates how the line spectrum of a rectangular pulse train changes as the interval between individual pulses, T, is increased while the pulse width τ remains unchanged. The spectral lines move closer together, and the amplitudes of the individual components decrease. Note, however, that the *general* form of the envelope has not changed. Its height decreases in proportion to the increase in T, but the frequencies at which it becomes zero, which depend only on the pulse width and not the pulse spacing, are unchanged.

An analytical expression for the envelopes of the line spectra of Figure 3.3 can be obtained from the Fourier series after a little manipulation. The coefficients, which I shall denote A_n, of the individual terms in the cosine series are given by the expression

$$A_n = \frac{2V \sin (n\pi\tau/T)}{n\pi}$$

for positive integral values of n. Similarly, the corresponding coefficients a_m of the exponential terms in the double-sided spectral representation are just half of these values, and are hence given by

$$a_m = \frac{V \sin (m\pi\tau/T)}{m\pi}$$

where in this case m can be any positive or negative integer (but not zero, which would be the dc term).

I was careful to refer to these expressions as coefficients, and not amplitudes because, as already noted, their signs vary according to the value of n or m. The amplitude of the individual double-sided components is therefore given by $|a_m|$, and the phase is either 0 or $\pm 180°$ according to the sign of the coefficient.

To obtain an expression for the spectral envelope I first multiply the numerator and denominator of the previous expression by τ/T and write the coefficient of the mth term as

$$a_m = \frac{V\tau}{T} \frac{\sin (m\pi\tau/T)}{m\pi\tau/T}$$

My reason for doing this is that I have now manipulated the second part of the expression into the form $(\sin x)/x$ where x in this case is $m\pi\tau/T$. The function

$$f(x) = \frac{\sin x}{x}$$

plays a very special role when modelling signals, and its graph is sketched in Figure 3.4. Note that $f(x) = 0$ for $x = n\pi$, and that the 'side lobes' decrease rapidly as x increases, as would be expected from the form of $f(x)$. Note also that $(\sin x)/x = 1$ when $x = 0$. This can be shown quite easily by expressing $\sin x$ as a series:

$$\sin x = x - \frac{x^3}{3!} + \frac{x^5}{5!} - \frac{x^7}{7!} + \cdots$$

and dividing each term by x, giving

$$\frac{\sin x}{x} = 1 - \frac{x^2}{3!} + \frac{x^4}{5!} - \frac{x^6}{7!} + \cdots$$

Hence

$$\lim_{x \to 0} \frac{\sin x}{x} = 1$$

The term amplitude is normally reserved for the (positive) peak value of a sinusoid. For instance, the amplitude of the sinusoid $A \cos (\omega t + \theta)$ is A.

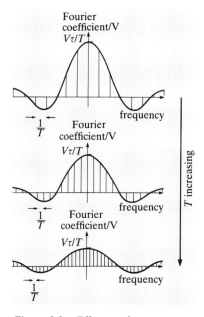

Figure 3.3 Effect on the spectrum of increasing pulse separation T

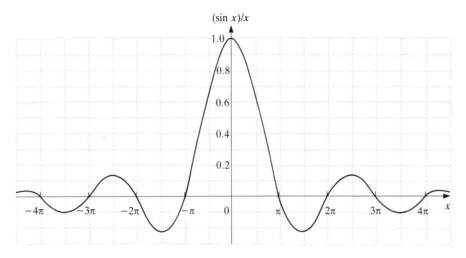

Figure 3.4 *The (sin x)/x function*

From the general shape of $f(x) = (\sin x)/x$ you can see the similarity of this function to the envelope of the line spectra of Figure 3.3. To obtain a precise mathematical expression for the envelope, however, we need a function of frequency $A(f)$, such that whenever $f = m/T$ (the frequencies of the spectral lines) the value of $A(f)$ is equal to a_m, and furthermore whenever f is an integral multiple of $1/\tau$, the value of $A(f)$ is zero.

SAQ 3.1 Using Figure 3.4 as a guide, sketch the graph of

$$A(f) = \frac{V\tau}{T} \frac{\sin(\pi\tau f)}{\pi\tau f}$$

as a function of f, and show that it has the required properties to represent the envelope of the line spectrum of the periodic pulse train.

It is as well at this point to stop for a moment and recall the aim of this whole exercise: to obtain a spectral representation of an isolated rectangular pulse. So far we have obtained an expression for the spectral envelope of a pulse train, and we have noted that, as the separation between pulses is increased, the lines get closer together, and the amplitude of the envelope shrinks. This was illustrated in Figure 3.3. To avoid this shrinking spectral envelope as the pulse spacing is increased indefinitely, we can introduce a new spectral variable $G(f)$ in place of $A(f)$, where $G(f)$ is defined by the expression:

$$G(f) = T \times A(f) = V\tau \frac{\sin(\pi\tau f)}{\pi\tau f}$$

☐ What are the units of $G(f)$ if the original pulse amplitude is given in volts? What is the value of $G(0)$, and what physical property of the pulses does it represent?

■ If the original pulse amplitude is in volts, then so are the amplitudes of the Fourier components of the pulse train, and so is the envelope function $A(f)$. The units of $G(f)$ are therefore volt seconds (V s). (A similar conclusion can be drawn from the analytic expression for $G(f)$.) Substituting $f = 0$ gives $G(0) = V\tau$, the 'area' or 'strength' of one individual pulse.

We can treat $G(f)$ as a normalised envelope function, which is independent of T (unlike $A(f)$) and which remains unchanged even as the spacing between the individual pulses is increased, as shown in Figure 3.5. The relevance of the new function $G(f)$ to modelling an isolated pulse is demonstrated particularly clearly by comparing $G(f)$ with $A(f)$ for $f = 0$. $G(0)$ is the area or strength of a single pulse, whereas $A(0)$ for this particular pulse train is the mean value or dc component.

Now at last we can derive a spectral representation of an isolated rectangular pulse. One way of presenting the argument runs as follows. The pulse train itself could be used as a model of an isolated pulse over any observation time less than the pulse repetition interval T. Within such an observation time the section of the pulse train is indistinguishable from an isolated pulse. Outside the observation 'window', however, the model is not

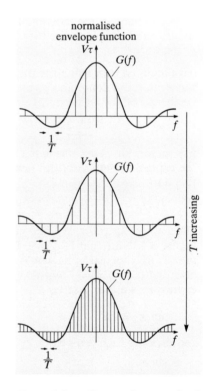

Figure 3.5 *Effect on the normalised spectrum of increasing pulse separation T*

22

valid, and this fact is reflected in the spectrum, which is still that of the complete periodic signal with a spacing between lines depending on T. Gradually increasing the repetition interval means that the model remains valid for longer and longer observation times: the spacing $1/T$ of the individual components in the spectrum, however, becomes narrower and narrower. If the repetition interval T is increased indefinitely, it is no longer possible to distinguish between the individual Fourier components. **In the limit of an *isolated* rectangular pulse, the spectral function $G(f)$ represents a *continuous* distribution of frequency components,** as shown in Figure 3.6. Such a continuous distribution $G(f)$ is known as the Fourier transform of the original pulse, and is a unique representation of it, just as a Fourier series is a unique representation of a periodic signal.

Admittedly, it is rather more difficult to attach a physical meaning to a continuous spectrum than to a line spectrum. The individual lines of the latter represent sinusoidal components in the periodic signal which could be identified experimentally by means of suitable band-pass filters. In the case of a continuous spectrum, however, it is impossible to identify any individual sinusoidal component. A continuous spectrum has to be interpreted in a rather different way, as illustrated by Figure 3.7 for a general spectrum. The figure indicates how the *area* of such a spectrum between two frequencies can be thought of as a measure of the contribution of that particular range of frequencies to the overall signal. Because of this property, the function $G(f)$ is also sometimes known as the *spectral density* and the units are expressed in volts per hertz (V Hz^{-1}). This interpretation can be given mathematical precision, although I shall not go into the details here. It is worth noting, however, that the units of this interpretation, volts per hertz, are consistent with the units volt seconds derived above.

The spectrum of a periodic signal always consists of distinct spectral lines, while the spectrum of an isolated pulse is always a continuous distribution of spectral components. In general, such a continuous spectrum, like a line spectrum, has both amplitude and phase terms. Mathematically this is reflected in a spectral density function $G(f)$ which, for a pulse of arbitrary shape, can take on complex values. In such a case $|G(f)|$ represents the continuous amplitude spectrum and $\angle G(f) = \phi(f)$ represents the continuous phase spectrum.

For an even pulse, such as the rectangular pulse drawn symmetrically about $t = 0$, $G(f)$ is real, and can be represented on a single diagram. A negative value of $G(f)$ for a particular frequency indicates that $\phi(f)$ has a value of $\pm\pi$ rad for that particular frequency – rather like a negative coefficient in a Fourier series. In this block I shall not be concerned with the phase spectra of pulses, although in some applications phase considerations are extremely important. All the pulses discussed in this block will be even, with real spectra.

The theoretical development I have just outlined is subtle, and you may have found it difficult. The best way to become familiar with the idea of a continuous spectrum is to use it in exercises. You should not go on to subsection 3.2 of this block without attempting the following SAQs conscientiously. These SAQs are aimed at giving you practice in switching easily between the time domain and frequency domain models of pulses, a skill which is vital if you are to be able to make practical use of such models.

SAQ 3.2   Sketch the spectrum $G(f)$ of each of the pulses shown in Figure 3.8. Label the numerical values of the zero crossings and the height of the spectrum at $f = 0$.

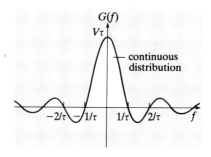

Figure 3.6   *A continuous distribution of spectral components*

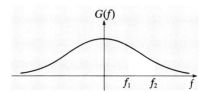

Figure 3.7   *Interpretation of a spectral density function. The white area has the dimensions of voltage*

This interpretation is very similar to the interpretation of a general frequency response function $H(f)$ in terms of amplitude ratio and phase shift, as described in Section 2. Exactly the same type of mathematical model can represent either a linear system frequency response, or a pulse spectrum.

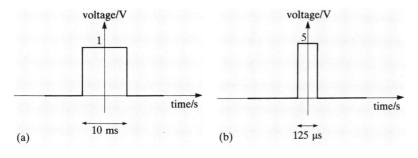

(a)   (b)

Figure 3.8   *Pulses for SAQ 3.2*

SAQ 3.3 Sketch the pulses corresponding to the spectra of Figure 3.9. Label the numerical values of the pulse heights and widths. (Assume in each case that the spectrum is of the form $(\sin x)/x$.)

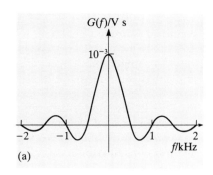

(a)

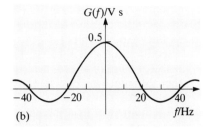

(b)

Figure 3.9 *Spectra for SAQ 3.3*

3.2 Input–output relationships

The continuous spectrum of a pulse can be used, in conjunction with a frequency response model of a linear communications channel, to evaluate the effects of the channel on a single transmitted pulse. The general idea is very similar to the use of Fourier series for periodic signals, and is illustrated in Figure 3.10. For a periodic signal, the effect of the channel can be represented as an amplitude change and phase shift for each Fourier component, as shown in part (a) of the figure. Suppose that the channel has an arbitrary frequency response denoted at any frequency f by the amplitude ratio $|H(f)|$ and phase characteristic $\theta(f) = \angle H(f)$. Then, in the steady state, a transmitted Fourier component at a frequency f, with input amplitude A_i and input phase angle ϕ_i, will be received as a sinusoid at the same frequency, but with output amplitude and phase A_o and ϕ_o such that

$$A_o = A_i \times |H(f)|$$

and

$$\phi_o = \phi_i + \theta(f)$$

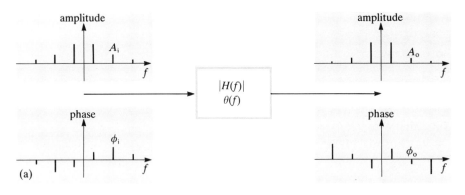

(a)

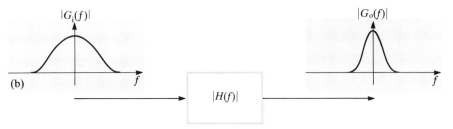

(b)

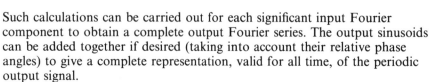

Figure 3.10 *Input–output relationships in the frequency domain: (a) a periodic signal; (b) a pulse*

Such calculations can be carried out for each significant input Fourier component to obtain a complete output Fourier series. The output sinusoids can be added together if desired (taking into account their relative phase angles) to give a complete representation, valid for all time, of the periodic output signal.

A similar procedure applies in the case of a pulse, as illustrated in Figure 3.10(b). Only the amplitude spectrum of the pulse is illustrated, but for completeness suppose that the full input spectrum can be represented as continuous amplitude and phase functions $|G_i(f)|$ and $\phi_i(f)$. The effect of the channel on the complete continuous input spectrum can be calculated, and hence a complete continuous output spectrum obtained. The input–output relationships in this case are

$$|G_o(f)| = |G_i(f)| \times |H(f)|$$

and

$$\phi_o(f) = \phi_i(f) + \theta(f)$$

This simply expresses in mathematical notation the standard frequency response ideas tested earlier in SAQ 2.1.

24

As with the periodic signal, we multiply the amplitude functions, and add the phase terms.

☐ Look at Figure 3.6 again, which represents the complete spectrum $G(f)$ of an isolated rectangular pulse of width τ. Suppose that this pulse is transmitted through an ideal low-pass channel which passes frequencies up to $1/\tau$ unchanged, and completely removes all higher frequencies. Sketch the *amplitude* spectra of the input and output pulses.

■ The ideal low-pass channel would completely remove all the frequency components of the pulse above $1/\tau$ Hz. The input and output amplitude spectra are shown in Figure 3.11.

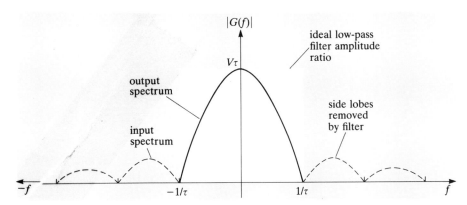

Figure 3.11   The effect of ideal low-pass filtering on a rectangular pulse spectrum

Note that in the example of this ITQ all the side lobes in the spectrum have been removed. This must have correspondingly serious consequences on the time domain shape, although it is impossible without further mathematical computation to say precisely what these consequences are. What we can say, however, is that if it is important to transmit pulses without distortion, such an arrangement of a rectangular pulse and a sharply bandlimited channel will not do. One approach to designing optimal pulse shapes is therefore to look for pulses with spectra appropriate to the frequency response characteristics of the channel.

3.3   Other pulse shapes

Although I have spent some time outlining the procedure by which the spectrum of an isolated rectangular pulse can be obtained, it is not important that you should remember the derivation. However, you do need to be able to make accurate sketches of spectra and pulses, as tested in SAQs 3.2 and 3.3, and you should also be able to make informed judgements about the general relationship between time domain characteristics of pulses and their spectra. SAQs 3.2 and 3.3 illustrated one such general relationship: the shorter the pulse, the greater the bandwidth of the corresponding spectrum.

There are many different precise definitions of bandwidth, but here I shall use the term loosely as some unspecified measure of the frequency range of a spectrum.

For the specific case of a rectangular pulse, as the pulse width is decreased, the first crossing of the frequency axis of the spectrum takes place at a higher frequency, and the side lobes of the spectrum remain significant at higher and higher frequencies. Sufficiently short pulses can even be treated as if they possessed a flat spectrum over a wide range of frequencies. This is illustrated by the amplitude spectra of Figure 3.12, where the pulses all have the same area $V\tau$, giving spectra of equal height at $f = 0$.

Because this general inverse relationship is so important, let me state it again as the first of a number of general properties of the time and frequency domains:

The shorter the pulse, the broader its spectrum.

The fact that a rectangular pulse has a spectrum which extends to arbitrarily high frequencies, with side lobes of considerable size, means that the energy of the pulse is distributed over a wide range of frequencies. If it is necessary to limit the bandwidth of the pulse being transmitted, then rectangular

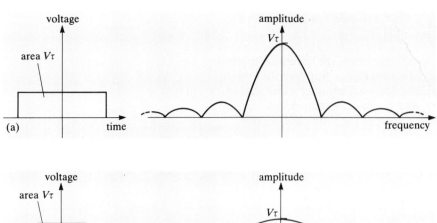

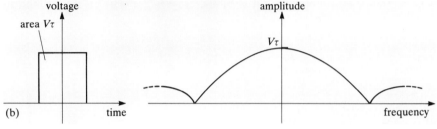

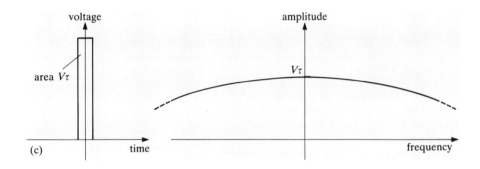

Figure 3.12 *Effect on the amplitude spectrum of decreasing the width of a rectangular pulse*

pulses may not be ideal. Figure 3.13 shows the spectra of some other pulse shapes, in comparison with that of a rectangular pulse. All the pulses have equal area and height so that it is easier to compare the spectra. This figure illustrates a second important relationship between the time and frequency domains. Compare the spectra of the rectangular pulse and the triangular pulse. The side lobes of the former decrease in size much more slowly than those of the latter, so the spectrum of the rectangular pulse extends to much higher frequencies than that of the triangular pulse. In fact, it can be shown that the heights of the lobes of the rectangular pulse spectrum are inversely proportional to frequency, whereas the heights of the triangular pulse side lobes are inversely proportional to the *square* of the frequency. The effect is even more pronounced for the third, 'raised cosine' pulse, that is, a pulse consisting of one cycle of a cosine wave raised by adding a dc level. The pulse spectrum is now almost completely limited to below $1/\tau$ Hz. A comparison of the shapes of the pulses themselves shows that the general 'smoothness' of the pulses increases as we go from rectangular to triangular to raised cosine. The rectangular pulse has two jump discontinuities: sudden changes in voltage level at the beginning and end of the pulse. The triangular pulse has no sudden jumps in voltage level, but the *slope* of the function changes suddenly three times. In the raised cosine case, even the *slope* of the pulse varies smoothly over the whole time interval. In fact, we have another general 'rule':

The side lobe heights are now inversely proportional to the *cube* of the frequency, and are so small that they can often be ignored for practical purposes.

Sudden changes in a pulse imply high frequencies in the corresponding spectrum.

SAQ 3.4   Figure 3.14 shows three pairs of pulses (a), (b), and (c). How would you expect the corresponding pairs of spectra to differ? Give sketches of amplitude spectra $|G(f)|$ where appropriate, labelling important numerical values of amplitude and frequency. (Hint: take care when using Figure 3.13 to note the appropriate pulse width.)

26

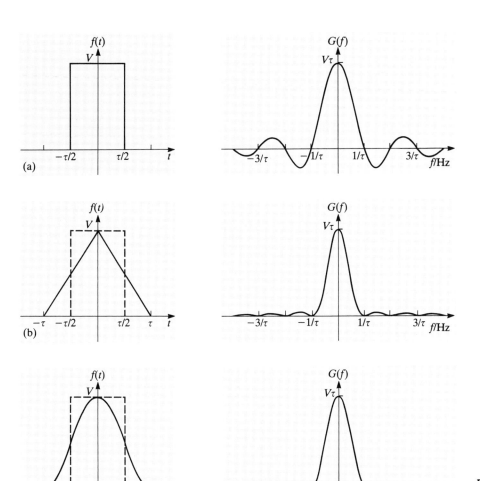

Figure 3.13 Spectra of (a) rectangular; (b) triangular; and (c) raised cosine pulses

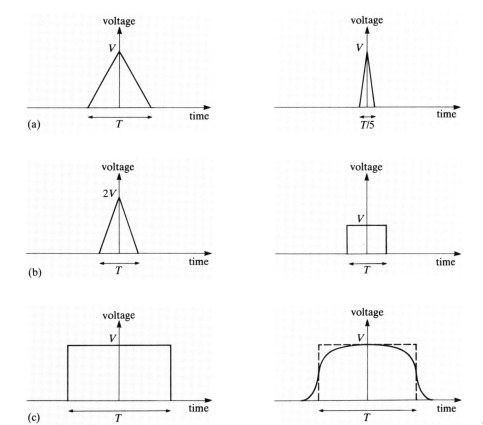

Figure 3.14 Pulses for SAQ 3.4

3.3.1 Transform pairs

As mentioned already, the relationship between a pulse and its spectrum is unique. The mathematical functions describing the two are said to form a *Fourier transform pair*. The pulses and spectra of Figure 3.13 illustrate three such transform pairs.

One of the interesting characteristics of such transform pairs is that the time domain and frequency domain functions can be interchanged, as illustrated in Figure 3.15. Not only does a rectangular pulse have a spectrum of the form $(\sin x)/x$, but also a 'pulse' shaped like the $(\sin x)/x$ function has a rectangular spectrum. Similarly, a raised cosine spectrum corresponds to the pulse shape shown.

Fourier transform pair

The pulse corresponding to the raised cosine spectrum is itself very similar in shape to a raised cosine. As noted above, for this particular shape, the side lobes die away so quickly that they can often be neglected. Incidentally, note that the perfect symmetry between Figures 3.13 and 3.15 is possible only when using double-sided spectra. This is one of the advantages of the double-sided representation.

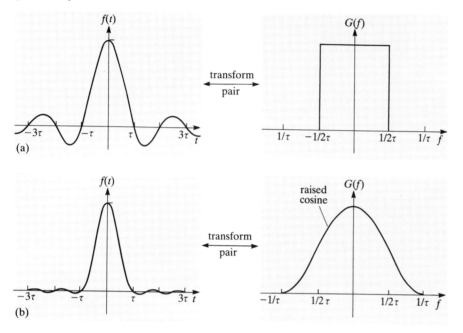

Figure 3.15 *Pulses with (a) rectangular and (b) raised cosine spectra*

A 'pulse' shaped like $(\sin x)/x$ is, of course, a mathematical abstraction: no physically occurring pulse could have precisely this shape. For example, in the sketches of Figure 3.15, both 'pulses' theoretically extend over the range $-\infty < t < +\infty$. Any physically realisable waveform, however, must have a well-defined beginning: even if we delay the pulse in time it can never have the precise mathematical form implied by the Fourier transform pair. Similarly, no physical signal can have a perfectly rectangular amplitude spectrum: there must be a smoother transition in the cut-off region. Such considerations, however, do not detract from the value of mathematical idealisations like these for modelling purposes. For example, although a perfectly rectangular spectrum cannot exist physically, it can be approached in practice when filters with very sharp cut-offs are used in telecommunications systems. So once we possess an idealised model of the type developed in this section, it is relatively straightforward to model many practical situations, particularly when, as is often the case in engineering design, we are concerned with worst-case estimates of system behaviour.

Of course, even perfectly square or triangular pulses are also mathematical idealisations. Again they can never be realised precisely, even though they are 'bounded in time', so do not extend over indefinitely great intervals.

I shall ask you simply to accept the inverse relationship between the Fourier transform pairs depicted in Figures 3.13 and 3.15, and I shall not attempt to justify it here. I mention it primarily because it is an illustration of a third general relationship between frequency spectra and their corresponding time domain signals. Note that the $(\sin x)/x$ 'pulse', which corresponds to a perfectly rectangular amplitude spectrum, is highly oscillatory. The pulse corresponding to the raised cosine spectrum, in contrast, is much less oscillatory; as mentioned before, its ripples can often be completely ignored. Figure 3.15 is in fact an illustration of another general correspondence, this time between sharp changes in the frequency domain and oscillations or 'ringing' in the time domain. So we have our third general 'rule':

Sudden changes in a spectrum imply oscillatory behaviour in the corresponding signal.

Figures 3.13 and 3.15, together with these three general 'rules' are the essence of what you need to know about pulses and their spectra. The unique relationship between a pulse shape and its spectrum, and between channel frequency response and time domain behaviour, are of vital importance in telecommunications engineering. They provide a modelling framework for designing systems in which the digital signals used to code information are properly matched to the channels through which they are transmitted. In particular the three 'rules' just presented sum up many of the compromises inherent in telecommunications. For example, the first rule implies that if we wish to transmit information at high rates, with corresponding rapid changes in the time domain, we have to accept that wide bandwidths will be required. Similarly, the other rules illustrate the trade-offs between pulse shape and bandwidth, and between the use of sharp filters (which may be desirable to use available bandwidth effectively) and the generation of oscillatory waveforms (which may be undesirable for other reasons). Such compromises and trade-offs will form a recurrent theme of this course.

3.4 Summary

The spectrum of an isolated pulse, unlike that of a periodic signal, is a continuous distribution of components, in which individual frequencies cannot be identified. Such continuous spectra, like line spectra, can be used in conjunction with the frequency response of a linear system to relate input and output signals. This frequency domain technique is a convenient approach to modelling the behaviour of digital telecommunication channels, and an alternative to summing the response of the system to individual signalling elements.

The equivalence between time domain and frequency domain models means that particular features of the one model imply corresponding features of the other. In particular:

1 The shorter a pulse, the broader its spectrum.

2 Sudden changes in a signal imply high frequencies in its spectrum.

3 Sudden changes in a spectrum imply oscillatory behaviour in the corresponding signal.

Naturally, these very broad 'rules' need to be interpreted carefully in the light of individual circumstances.

The spectra of a number of important idealised pulses were introduced: the rectangular pulse, the triangular pulse and the raised cosine pulse (Figure 3.13); and the pulses with rectangular and raised cosine *spectra* (Figure 3.15). Although these pulses are all mathematical abstractions, they provide useful idealisations for modelling practical systems and signals.

4 ASPECTS OF DIGITAL SIGNAL TRANSMISSION

In this section I shall look briefly at the transmission of digital signals in the light of the spectral properties discussed in Sections 2 and 3. I aim to illustrate the way in which the rather theoretical material of the previous sections can be applied; and to introduce the topic of digital signal transmission in preparation for later parts of the course.

To begin with, look at Figure 4.1, which is a repeat of Figure 2.1. I shall use this figure as a starting point for a discussion of a number of general aspects of the transmission process. I shall first consider threshold detection, and the nature of the most desirable shape for the received pulses of waveform C. I shall then examine some elementary coding aspects of systems for transmitting digital data over distances greater than a few hundred metres.

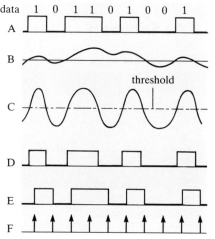

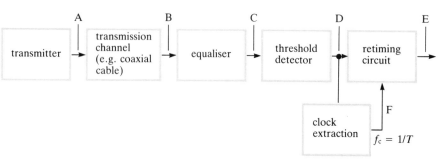

Figure 4.1 *Part of a binary digital transmission system (repeat of Figure 2.1)*

4.1 Threshold detection

A detection process like that of Figure 4.1 takes place at every receiver of a digital signal. As noted before, it amounts to a decision made at regular intervals of time about the state of the incoming signal. For a digital signal whose different states are represented by different voltage levels, the decision process involves placing the incoming signal in one of a number of voltage bands, as shown in Figure 4.2 for a quaternary voltage level system. If, for example, the signal were sampled and found to have a voltage between V_2 and V_3, then state C would be assumed.

For a binary system, such a decision process reduces to determining whether the signal voltage is above or below a single threshold level V_t, as shown in Figure 4.3. Assuming positive logic, if the incoming voltage is above the threshold then state 1 is assumed; if it is below the threshold then state 0 is assumed. To minimise errors, the level of the threshold must be accurately maintained, and the peaks and troughs of the received, distorted signal should correlate well with the transmitted binary pattern.

4.2 Intersymbol interference

This last point brings me to an important aspect of threshold detection. Consider waveform C of Figure 4.1. Although each original data pulse has been rounded during transmission, the binary 1s and 0s are still clearly distinguishable: the peaks and troughs of the waveform correspond to the transmitted binary 1s and 0s. In particular, individual pulses have not been broadened to the extent that they interfere with decisions about adjacent signalling elements. Now contrast this with the situation shown in Figure 4.4, which illustrates a phenomenon known as *intersymbol interference*, or *ISI*. In this figure, the 'tails' of the received binary 1 pulses have extended so far into

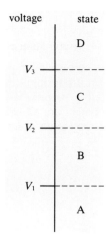

Figure 4.2 *Threshold detection in a quaternary voltage level system*

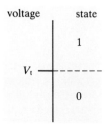

Figure 4.3 *Threshold detection in a binary system*

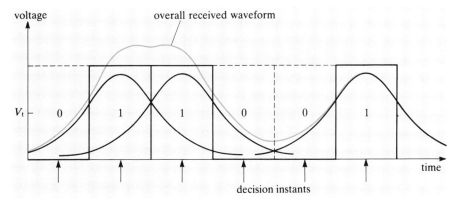

voltage

overall received waveform

V_t — 0 | 1 | 1 | 0 | 0 | 1

time

decision instants

As usual I have assumed linear phase and have normalised the diagram to zero channel delay, which is why the 'tails' extend into time slots on both sides of a given decision point.

Figure 4.4   *Intersymbol interference*

the adjacent time slots that a detector sampling at regular intervals would detect a considerable signal level in the binary 0 positions. In the noise-free example shown, this would not in itself lead to misinterpretation of 0s and 1s, provided that the threshold level were correctly set. However, a comparatively small noise level or threshold error would be enough to cause such a misinterpretation.

A convenient way of estimating the likely error arising from intersymbol interference is illustrated by Figures 4.5 and 4.6. Part (a) of Figure 4.5 shows a received, distorted binary waveform. In part (b) the signal has been separated into time segments each corresponding to one signalling element, and a central cross-hair has been added to each time segment to indicate both the threshold level and the decision instant. In a noise-free system with little ISI the curve representing the signal will be located well clear of the cross-hair for all time segments, as is the case here. Figure 4.6 shows the superposition of all such individual time segments to give a composite representation. What is important is not the shape of these superimposed waveforms, but how close any of the waveforms are to the central cross-hair, since a close approach to the ideal decision point means an increased likelihood of error. The size of the clear area around the cross-hair can in fact be used to estimate directly the likely error rate in the system.

intersymbol interference (ISI)

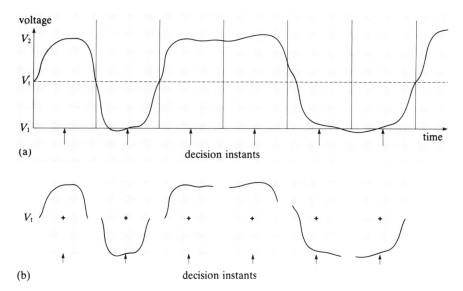

voltage

V_2

V_t

V_1

time

(a)   decision instants

V_t +   +   +   +   +   +

(b)   decision instants

Figure 4.5   *Separating a binary signal into successive signalling elements*

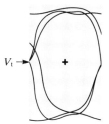

V_t →   +

Figure 4.6   *Building up an eye diagram by superposition*

Because of the general appearance of Figure 4.6, such a diagram is known as an *eye diagram*. One of the advantages of the eye diagram is that it can be obtained from a received digital waveform very easily using an oscilloscope. The oscilloscope is triggered by the receiver clock pulses, and the waveforms received in successive time slots are automatically superimposed on the oscilloscope screen. The area of the eye opening can also be estimated easily from the graticule of the scope.

eye diagram

4.2.1 Pulse shaping

It should be clear from the preceding discussion that intersymbol interference is an important consideration in digital signal transmission. The characteristics of the transmission link – by which I mean the combination of transmitter, channel and receiver – must be carefully designed so that individual pulses have the minimum possible effect at adjacent decision instants. There would seem to be two ways to minimise the ISI illustrated in Figure 4.4. Either the signalling speed can simply be reduced, so that the tails of the pulses do not overlap significantly, or the shape of the received pulses can be tailored so that their contribution to the detected signal level at adjacent decision instants is negligible. Clearly, the second approach offers the greater potential for efficient transmission.

One of the idealised pulse shapes discussed in the previous section has particularly desirable features with respect to intersymbol interference, namely, the pulse of Figure 3.15(b) with the raised cosine *spectrum*. Figure 4.7 is a reminder of the shape of this pulse, together with its spectrum. Note particularly the relationship between the nominal pulse width $2T$s and the width of its spectrum $1/T$ Hz.

A bandlimited double-sided spectrum extending from $-f$ to $+f$ has a width of f.

I am now using T in place of τ of Figure 3.15(b).

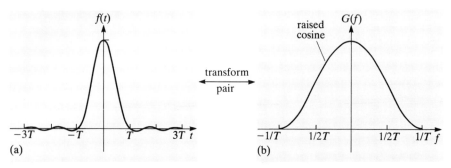

Figure 4.7 *Raised cosine spectrum and corresponding pulse. Note that the pulse is shown in (a), and the spectrum in (b)*

The pulse of Figure 4.7 has been drawn symmetrically about the time origin, like all the pulses of the previous section. This is for mathematical convenience: a similar pulse delayed in time would have an identical amplitude spectrum (although the phase spectrum would differ). The important point to note is that the pulse has almost completely died away T seconds after its maximum. So if we could arrange for the input to the threshold detector to approximate to Figure 4.7(a), then we could transmit data at a rate of one signalling element every T seconds (a data rate of $1/T$ bits s^{-1} for a binary system) with negligible intersymbol interference. This is illustrated in Figure 4.8. For decision instants regularly spaced at intervals of T seconds, a pulse has negligible effect outside its own particular time slot.

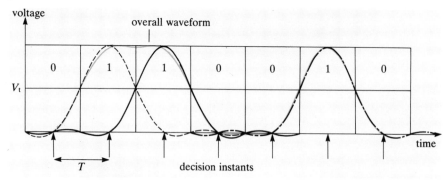

Figure 4.8 *Reducing intersymbol interference using raised cosine spectrum pulses*

In many textbook discussions much is made of the theoretical result that a pulse with a perfect raised cosine spectrum is zero at all decision instants outside its own time slot. (This result can be proved mathematically by deriving the Fourier transform of the raised cosine spectrum.) More important for practical purposes, however, are two other characteristics:

● As already noted, the pulse has a very small value T seconds or more from its maximum. So even if the timing of the decision instants is not perfectly regular, there will be little ISI.

● A raised cosine spectrum, unlike the spectra of some other pulses with theoretically zero ISI, can be reasonably well approximated in practice.

4.2.2 Implications for telecommunication systems

In the previous discussion I have referred to 'tailoring the shape of received pulses' and to the 'overall pulse response of the channel'. This is because it is the *received* pulses which suffer from intersymbol interference, and the shape of these received pulses will be affected by the precise shape transmitted, the frequency response of the channel, and any filtering in the receiver before threshold detection. I now want to look at pulse shaping in this general context.

As a starting point, assume that the channel has a completely flat response over the range of frequencies of interest, and that the transmitter shapes the transmitted pulses into an approximation to the desirable form of Figure 4.7(a). With a flat channel response which introduces neither amplitude nor phase distortion, these pulses will arrive unchanged at the receiver, thus minimising ISI as described above. What would be the minimum channel bandwidth required under these conditions? As Figure 4.7(b) shows, the spectrum of a pulse of width $2T$s extends to $1/T$ Hz, and this spectrum must be passed unchanged by the channel. Hence the minimum channel bandwidth is also $1/T$ Hz.

Since signalling without ISI can take place at a maximum rate of $1/T$ states s^{-1} for a binary system, we note that **the maximum signalling rate using 'raised cosine' shaping is equal to the channel bandwidth.**

☐ How does this result relate to the maximum theoretical rate presented in Section 2.2?

■ The theoretical result of Section 2.2 states a maximum signalling rate of $2B$ states s^{-1} over a channel of bandwidth B Hz. The raised cosine strategy therefore requires twice the theoretical minimum bandwidth. This is the price paid for the desirable ISI properties of the raised cosine spectrum.

In general, the channel frequency response will not be perfectly flat over the bandwidth of the transmitted pulse, and it may be desirable to carry out some additional signal processing at the receiver. The general case can be represented, in frequency domain terms, by Figure 4.9, where $G_T(f)$ represents the spectrum of the transmitted pulse (now not necessarily raised cosine), $C(f)$ the channel frequency response and $G_R(f)$ the frequency response of the signal processing (filtering, equalisation) at the receiver. I have also shown additive noise in the figure. If we require raised cosine *received* pulses in this general case then, neglecting noise for a moment, the design problem is to ensure that the spectrum of the received pulse ($G_T(f) \times C(f) \times G_R(f)$ in frequency domain terms) is of the raised cosine form of Figure 4.7. As far as bandwidth requirements are concerned, the situation is equivalent to the case of a flat channel and raised cosine shaping of the transmitted pulse. An overall bandwidth of $1/T$ Hz is still necessary if the received pulse of width $2T$s is to have the raised cosine spectrum.

In fact, there is a whole family of spectra based on the 'raised cosine' shape, in which bandwidth requirements can be traded off against desirable ISI properties. Discussion of these other raised cosine spectra is beyond the scope of this course, but they are of considerable practical importance. Details can be found in Peebles (1987) and Schwartz (1980).

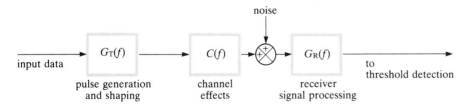

Figure 4.9 *Frequency domain representation of a digital telecommunication link*

So far in this discussion I have assumed that ISI is the major problem causing errors in the transmission system. Sometimes this is the case, but often noise is just as important or even more so. In the general case the design aim is to choose $G_T(f)$, $C(f)$ and $G_R(f)$ so that the overall error rate due to noise and/or ISI is minimised. Often there is little scope for modifying the characteristics of the channel itself, so the precise forms of $G_T(f)$ and $G_R(f)$ take on a great significance. As you will see later in the course there is an optimum way of 'matching' $G_T(f)$ and $G_R(f)$ to maximise signal-to-noise ratio at the receiver, and hence reduce error rates.

4.3 Coding aspects

To conclude this section I want to look at some of the ways that the characteristics of the transmission channel can affect the choice of coding schemes for digital data. Many transmission links (particularly those used for long-distance data transmission rather than local networks) incorporate transformers and series capacitors, and will effectively block any dc component in a message signal. You have already seen examples of binary waveforms with and without dc components in Section 2, where it was noted that any signal with zero average value has a zero dc component. Part of such a zero-mean bipolar binary waveform is shown in its transmitted form in Figure 4.10. Difficulties will still be encountered, however, if such a signal is passed through a channel having zero dc response. Any long runs of 1s and 0s will result in the 'droop' of the transmitted voltage level, as illustrated in Figure 4.11.

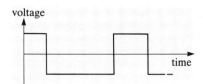

Figure 4.10 *Part of a zero-mean bipolar waveform*

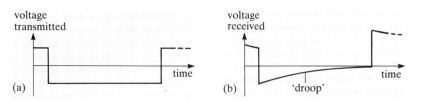

Figure 4.11 *Droop caused by ac coupling*

One coding scheme which avoids such 'droop' is known as *alternate mark inversion (AMI)*. In AMI, zero volts is used to represent binary 0, and binary 1s are represented using alternate equal positive and negative voltages. A typical AMI waveform is illustrated in Figure 4.12.

4.3.1 Timing extraction

Alternate mark inversion is an example of how an unwanted component, in this case dc, can be removed from a signal without adversely affecting the message being transmitted. In other circumstances, however, we may wish to ensure that certain frequency components are indeed present. For example, in a synchronous transmission system, the receiver needs to be able to lock on to the data rate in order to time the threshold decision instants correctly. The process of deriving a timing frequency at the data rate is often known as *timing* or *clock extraction*, and can be carried out in two basic ways. The first is to use a coding scheme which will ensure a substantial frequency component in the data stream at the desired data rate. This can then be filtered out and used to time a clock signal directly. Alternatively, a frequency component at some related frequency can be identified and extracted, and then processed in a non-linear way to derive the required timing waveform. In each case the vital requirement is that the transmitted waveform should always contain sufficiently frequent transitions between signalling states for the clock frequency to be extracted.

> **SAQ 4.1**   Consider the 'worst-case' messages ... 10101010 ... for a zero-mean bipolar waveform, and ... 11111111 ... for an AMI waveform. Do either of the corresponding line spectra contain a significant frequency component at the data rate?

As the above SAQ showed, neither the bipolar nor the AMI waveform possesses a component at the data rate. In fact, the spectrum of each is concentrated at frequencies below the data rate even for these worst-case waveforms, which represent the fastest transitions between states. A simple form of non-linear processing can generate the required frequency, however. One technique is first to differentiate an AMI waveform, thus generating a series of 'spikes', one for each transition. This is illustrated in Figure 4.13(a) and (b) for the message signal ... 11111111 ... Although the differentiated signal still possesses no data rate component, subsequent full-wave rectification puts matters right, as illustrated in Figure 4.13(c). Figure 4.14 shows a simple practical circuit, where a high-pass filter with a suitably short time constant performs approximate differentiation, and the diode bridge arrangement rectifies the differentiated signal.

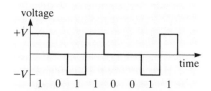

Figure 4.12 *Part of an AMI waveform*

alternate mark inversion (AMI)
The expression derives from the use of the old telegraphy terms *mark* and *space* to mean binary 1 and 0 respectively.

timing extraction

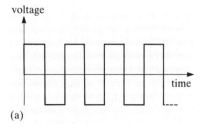

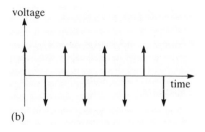

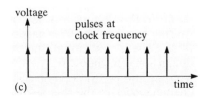

Figure 4.13 *Principle of timing extraction for an AMI signal: (a) AMI; (b) differentiated; (c) rectified*

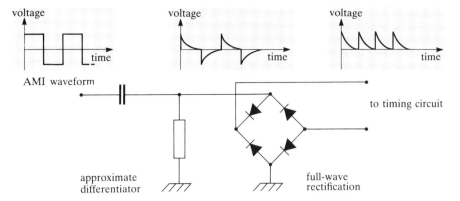

Figure 4.14 *A simple circuit for timing extraction*

☐   The circuit of Figure 4.14 carries out approximate differentiation followed by full-wave rectification. Which is the non-linear process?

■   Rectification. Differentiation (or its approximation, high-pass filtering) produces no new frequency components (and also obeys the principle of superposition). Full-wave rectification, however, effectively doubles the fundamental frequency of the signal. (Compare the fundamental frequencies of Figures 4.13(b) and (c).)

SAQ 4.2   In what circumstances would an AMI waveform not result in a strong data rate component after differentiation and rectification?

SAQ 4.2 illustrates the general point mentioned earlier: the necessity for frequent transitions between states if a timing waveform is to be extracted from a digital signal. A long run of 0s in AMI can result in insufficient transitions to give a timing waveform, and synchronisation could hence be lost. A modification of AMI which overcomes this difficulty, and which is one code recommended by CCITT, is known as *HDB3* (High Density Bipolar with substitution after three 0s). In this coding scheme, up to three consecutive 0s are transmitted in the usual way, as zero volts, but a fourth is not. Instead, it is coded as a 1, *but with a polarity identical to, rather than opposite to, the preceding transmitted binary 1.* This enables the receiver to recognise it as a violation of the alternating polarity rule, and hence correctly identify it as a binary 0 and not a 1.

AMI and HDB3 are examples of *line codes*, since they are expressly designed to match the properties of the digital signal actually transmitted to particular features of the line. In a public network, line coding is carried out by the appropriate telecommunications authority. As you will see in a later block, line codes also enable certain errors to be detected and corrected, although they may be used in addition to other coding specifically designed for error detection and correction. The various types of coding used in communication systems will be taken up in much more detail later in the course.

Non-linear processing produces components in the output which are *not* present in the input. Appropriate processing can therefore generate the desired clock frequency even when the original signal does not possess such a component.

HDB3
The full coding rules for HDB3 are rather more complex than indicated here. The overall scheme is designed to maintain certain general signal properties even after the substitution of 1s for particular 0s.

line codes

4.4 Summary

If pulses are distorted during transmission to the extent that they interfere with threshold detection for adjacent signalling elements, then intersymbol interference (ISI) is said to occur. The eye diagram is a useful way of measuring the degree of ISI in a transmission system.

Pulse shaping can be used to reduce ISI. A pulse with particularly desirable properties is the one with a raised cosine spectrum, introduced in Section 3. Such a pulse can be approximated in practice by means of pulse shaping at the transmitter, filters in the receiver, or a combination of both. The maximum signalling rate using raised cosine shaping is equal to the channel bandwidth – a signalling rate equal to one half of the theoretical maximum.

It is usually necessary to ensure that the transmitted digital signal possesses certain other general properties in addition to favourable ISI characteristics. For long-distance data communication a zero dc component is normally required, and transitions between states must occur frequently enough for an accurate timing signal to be derived. Various line codes are used for this purpose; alternate mark inversion (AMI) and HDB3 are simple examples.

5 PULSE CODE MODULATION

So far in this block I have assumed that the signals to be transmitted have originated in digital form, as binary codes for communication between computers, for example. Often, however, we wish to transmit analogue signals using a digital transmission link. One of the most common examples is the transmission of telephone (or other) audio signals in this way by means of the technique known as *pulse code modulation* (*PCM*).

pulse code modulation (*PCM*)

The general principle of pulse code modulation is illustrated schematically in Figure 5.1. Instead of transmitting the continuous analogue signal directly, it is first sampled periodically, and the values of the individual samples are then transmitted as digital codes. (I have shown a binary digital waveform, but any type of digital signal could be used.) At the receiver the digital signal is decoded, and interpolation between samples is carried out in order to 'reconstruct' or recover the original message signal. It is convenient to analyse the process of pulse code modulation into three distinct stages: sampling; encoding and decoding; and reconstruction or signal recovery. In this section I shall consider these three stages in turn.

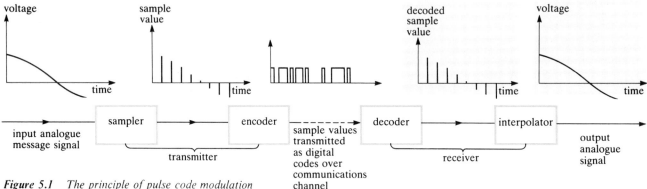

Figure 5.1   *The principle of pulse code modulation*

5.1 Sampling

Figure 5.2 illustrates a vitally important feature of the sampling process. In part (a) the message signal changes smoothly, without fluctuation, between sampling instants. As long as this is the case – and I shall quantify this proviso in a moment – smooth interpolation between the sample values will recover the message signal. Figure 5.2(b) shows a contrasting example, in which any attempt to reconstruct the original waveform simply by smooth interpolation would fail: the 'reconstructed' waveform does not reflect the fluctuation of the message signal between samples, and information has been lost. An even more extreme example is shown in Figure 5.2(c), where the interpolated waveform bears no resemblance to the original signal – it represents a completely different sinusoid. The general phenomenon is known as *aliasing*, and the improperly reconstructed sinusoid of Figure 5.2(c) is said to be a low-frequency alias of the original signal. Clearly, in order to be able to reconstruct a sampled signal properly, the sampling rate must be matched in some way to the frequency range of the original analogue message signal.

aliasing

The general problem of the transmission of information in sampled form was studied in detail in the late 1940s (Shannon, 1948). A simplified statement of Shannon's famous sampling theorem is as follows:

If the frequency components present in a continuous signal extend from 0 to B Hz, then the signal can be completely represented by, and reconstructed from, a sequence of equally spaced samples, provided that the sampling frequency exceeds $2B$ samples per second.

As Figure 5.2 clearly shows, the sampling process of part (c) violates the requirement of the sampling theorem: the sampling frequency is almost equal to the frequency of the message sinusoid, rather than at least twice as great. Hence the aliasing problem illustrated. A similar situation arises in (b), where the high-frequency fluctuations are well above half the sampling frequency.

This is a restricted version of the sampling theorem which, in a more general formulation, also applies to bandlimited signals which do *not* extend down to dc and to signals which are sampled at *irregular* intervals.

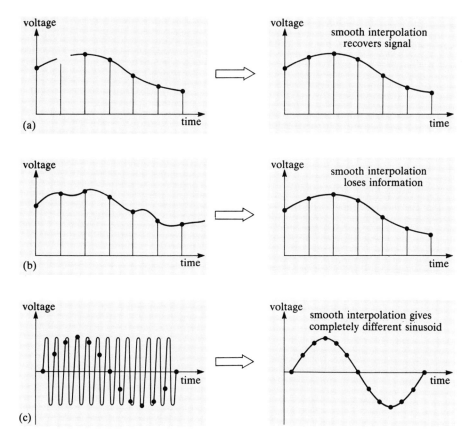

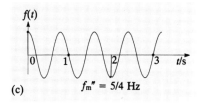

Figure 5.2 *The effect of sampling and smooth interpolation on three message signals*

5.1.1 Spectra of sampled signals

Just as both periodic signals and aperiodic pulses can be uniquely represented by their spectra, so a sampled signal also has a corresponding frequency domain description. I now want to outline a qualitative approach to the spectra of sampled signals. What follows is not a derivation, but simply a demonstration of the *plausibility* of the frequency domain model of a sampled signal.

Figure 5.2(c) illustrated how a single sequence of samples can represent more than one sinusoid. This gives us the clue to the frequency domain representation of such a sampled signal. Figure 5.3(a) shows a sinusoid with a period of 4 s sampled at a rate of once per second, that is, a message frequency $f_m = 1/4$ Hz and a sampling frequency $f_s = 1$ Hz. But what other sinusoids could have generated these samples? Figures 5.3(b) and (c) show that identical samples could have been taken from sinusoids with frequencies of $f_m' = 3/4$ Hz or $f_m'' = 5/4$ Hz.

☐ Are there any other possibilities? If so, what are they?

■ Making a few rough sketches should convince you that sinusoids with frequencies of 7/4 Hz and 9/4 Hz, 11/4 Hz and 13/4 Hz, and so on, would all give rise to the same sequence of sample values.

The sample values illustrated in Figure 5.3 have the potential to represent an infinite number of continuous sinusoids. This fact is reflected in the frequency domain model of a sampled signal. Figure 5.4 shows the amplitude spectrum corresponding to the samples of Figure 5.3. It includes not only the spectral lines of the original sinusoid, at $f = \pm 1/4$ Hz, but also an infinite set of equally spaced replicas of these lines, centred around multiples of the sampling frequency.

In Figure 5.4, the signal before sampling was sinusoidal, but exactly the same principle applies to more complex signals with line or continuous spectra. The spectrum of the sampled signal always consists of replicas of the original spectrum, centred around integral multiples of the sampling frequency. Figure 5.5 shows an example where the original signal has a continuous spectrum extending from 0 to f_B, and where the condition $f_B < f_s/2$ holds in accordance with the sampling theorem.

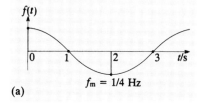

(a)

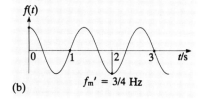

(b)

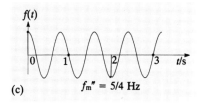

(c)

Figure 5.3 *A single sequence of samples taken from three different sinusoids*

Sampled signals also possess repeated phase spectra, although I shall not consider these here.

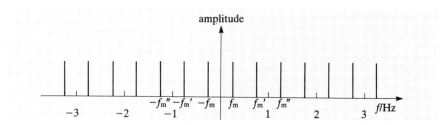

Figure 5.4 Amplitude spectrum of a sampled sinusoid

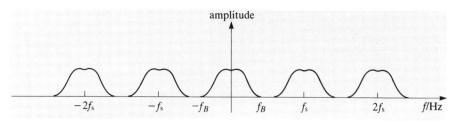

Figure 5.5 Amplitude spectrum of a general sampled signal

I have not attempted to quantify the heights of these lines, although in a full mathematical treatment this can be done. (They would not normally be identical to the heights of the original spectral lines.) Note that the bilateral representation of the message spectrum is necessary for the sampled version to have its infinite repeating form.

SAQ 5.1   A periodic signal, one cycle of which is shown in Figure 5.6(a), has the amplitude line spectrum shown in Figure 5.6(b). The signal is sampled at a frequency of 100 Hz. Sketch the amplitude spectrum of the sampled signal over the range -150 to $+150$ Hz.

All I have done so far is indicate the plausibility of a repeated spectrum model of a sampled signal, the justification being that the spectrum then contains all the frequencies that the particular sequence of samples can possibly represent. This model is highly idealised, and you may be wondering how it relates to actual digital systems. At this point therefore it is useful to introduce a *physical* model of the sampling process, still highly idealised but in a form which allows our abstraction to be related to practical systems.

Figure 5.7(a) shows the sampling process modelled as a simple switch. When the switch is in position A, the output signal is equal to the input analogue signal. When the switch is in position B, the output is 0 V. If we now assume that the switch is opened and closed periodically at intervals of T seconds, such that the time in the closed position is very much shorter than the time in the open position, the sampled signal can be represented as shown in Figure 5.7(b). In the limit of very short pulses the heights of the individual pulses represent the values of the analogue signal at the sampling instants, and the *sampling frequency* $f_s = 1/T$ Hz.

It can be shown that for very narrow pulses, the spectrum of a signal like that of Figure 5.7(b) approaches the form of Figure 5.5, that is, the spectrum of the analogue signal centred around multiples of the sampling frequency f_s. Again, I do not wish to go into the height of the sampled amplitude spectrum: it depends on the sampling interval and the 'strength' or area of the individual pulses.

The sampling process represented by Figure 5.7 can be thought of as the limiting case of *pulse amplitude modulation (PAM)*.

Systems do exist in which signals are transmitted as short pulses like Figure 5.7, but these are relatively uncommon. When I refer to such a waveform below it will be as a conceptual model of a sampled signal, where the individual pulses are considered to be very narrow compared with the sampling interval.

The PAM model is particularly useful since it illustrates in theory how a signal can be recovered from its samples, and also provides a context for interpreting the sampling theorem. Look at Figure 5.5 again, and assume that it represents the spectrum of a train of narrow pulses. At the low-frequency end of the spectrum is the spectrum of the original message signal. The message signal can therefore be recovered simply by means of a

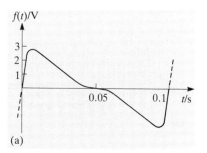

(a)

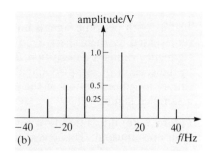

(b)

Figure 5.6 (a) Periodic signal and (b) its amplitude spectrum for SAQ 5.1

sampling frequency

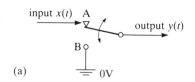

(a)

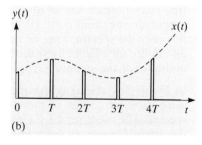

(b)

Figure 5.7 A switch model of the sampling process: (a) the sampler; and (b) the sampled output signal

suitable low-pass filter which passes all components up to f_B Hz unchanged, and completely removes the high-frequency replicas.

Suppose now that the sampling frequency is (a) increased and (b) decreased. The effect on the repeated spectrum in each case is shown in Figure 5.8. Increasing the sampling frequency (part (a) of the figure) simply increases the spacing between the replicas of the message signal: the original can still be recovered by simple low-pass filtering. In Figure 5.8(b) the sampling frequency has been decreased such that $f_B > f_s/2$. The repeated spectra now overlap, and aliasing occurs. In these circumstances the output of a low-pass filter would not be an accurate replica of the message signal. Once the spectra have overlapped as shown, it is impossible to recover the original spectrum by either low-pass filtering or indeed by any other means. This is entirely in accordance with the sampling theorem: a baseband signal with a bandwidth f_B must be sampled at a frequency of at least $2f_B$.

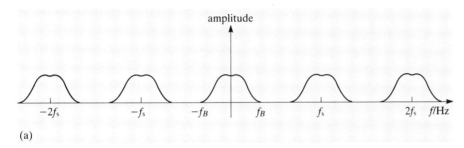

(a)

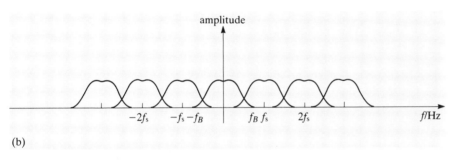

(b)

Figure 5.8 Effect in the frequency domain of (a) increasing and (b) decreasing the sampling rate

In any practical system, sampling rates are chosen to be somewhat higher than the theoretical minimum, to reduce demands on the cut-off characteristics of the filters used in the recovery process. For example, the spectrum of a telephone speech signal extends from about 300 Hz to 3.4 kHz, and is usually sampled at a frequency of 8 kHz for digital transmission instead of the minimum of $2 \times 3.4 = 6.8$ kHz. It is also usual to include a low-pass *anti-aliasing filter* before sampling an analogue message signal. The filter eliminates any unwanted high-frequency components, and hence ensures that the analogue signal sampled is indeed bandlimited as required.

One final point is worth making here, which will also be relevant when I discuss signal recovery in more detail. In pulse code modulation systems, electronic samplers are usually combined in practice with a *hold* device. This, as its name implies, holds the sampled value steady between sampling instants, so that conversion to a digital representation can take place unaffected by variations in the analogue input between sampling instants. This is illustrated in Figure 5.9. Nevertheless, the simple switch model of a sampler, and the associated pulse train model of a sampled signal, are valuable idealisations which reflect the essential feature of a sampled signal – namely, that it assumes the value of the analogue original *only at the sampling instants*, and not at any other moment in time.

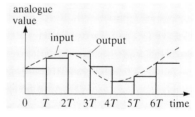

Figure 5.9 Action of a sample and hold device

Any real device, such as a capacitor used to 'hold' sample values, will take a certain time to change from one sampled value to another, so in practice the changes will not be the perfect steps illustrated.

5.2 Encoding and decoding

The sampled values of an analogue message signal cannot be transmitted exactly using binary codes of a finite word length. Before coding, therefore, each sample of an analogue message signal must be allocated to one of a finite number of *quantisation levels*, in a way very similar to normal analogue-to-digital conversion.

quantisation level

☐ How many quantisation levels can an 8-bit binary word represent? If the interval between adjacent quantisation levels is q volts, what is the difference between the top and bottom levels?

■ An 8-bit word can represent $2^8 = 256$ different states. So there are 256 different quantisation levels, and the difference between the top and bottom levels is $255q$ volts.

The quantisation process is illustrated in Figure 5.10, for a system using 4-bit words and hence 16 different quantisation levels. Each of these levels is allocated a 4-bit code. I have labelled the lowest level with the 'all-zeros' code, and the highest with the 'all-ones' code, although in practice, more complex coding systems are used as will be described in Section 6.

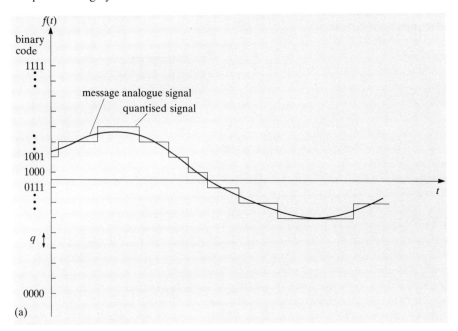

(a)

You should recall this figure from the *Introduction*, where the concepts of quantisation and digitisation were first introduced.

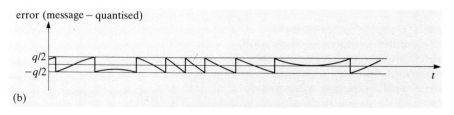

(b)

Figure 5.10 *(a) Quantisation using 16 discrete levels; (b) Error introduced by the quantisation process*

Because of the finite number of permissible levels, values cannot be encoded exactly but must be rounded up or down to the nearest level as appropriate. Figure 5.10(a) shows an analogue message signal together with its quantised version. If the levels are separated by q volts, then the maximum error introduced by the quantisation process is $q/2$, and the average error is zero. This is illustrated in part (b) of the figure, which is obtained by subtracting the quantised signal from the original message signal.

Note that a message signal could exceed the top or bottom levels by up to half a quantisation interval without the maximum error exceeding $q/2$. Beyond this, further distortion occurs at a result of saturation.

The error between the original and quantised signals is a fundamental limitation to the performance of a PCM system, since even a signal perfectly reconstructed from the transmitted digital codes will suffer from it. The effect is usually known as *quantisation distortion* or *quantisation noise*. Here, I want to describe briefly one particular consequence for PCM encoding and decoding.

quantisation distortion
quantisation noise

The amplitude of a typical telephone speech signal can vary enormously, both from one speaker to another and over the normal speaking range of a single individual. In fact, the range of variation from the 'whisper of a quiet speaker to the bellowing tones of a powerful speaker' (Schwartz, 1980) can be as great as 50 or 60 dB. Now, a dynamic range of 60 dB means that the ratio between the amplitude of the loudest signal V_l and softest V_s is given by the expression

$$60 = 20 \log (V_l/V_s)$$

that is, $V_1/V_s = 1000$. If we assume that V_s is of the order of one quantisation interval, then to cover the whole range of positive and negative signals with equal spacing we need at least 2000 distinct levels.

☐ What binary wordlength would be required to code 2000 levels?

■ $2^{10} = 1024$ and $2^{11} = 2048$. Therefore, 11-bit words would be required.

With equally spaced levels, the effect of quantisation noise (in relative terms) will be greater at the lower end of the signal range than at the upper end. Furthermore, since the very loudest sounds will occur infrequently, it is wasteful to provide high resolution (closely spaced levels) for these comparatively rare occasions. In fact, it is not necessary to use quantisation levels equally spaced over the whole range. It would seem reasonable (and it also fits in well with the way sound is perceived by human beings) to use levels which are closer together for low-intensity signals and further apart for louder sounds. In this way, some suitable measure of the quantisation error relative to the signal strength can be kept more or less constant over the whole range, while using a smaller number of levels. The levels are usually arranged in such a way that the *signal to quantisation-noise ratio* is approximately constant whatever the level of the speech signal. (Signal to quantisation-noise ratio is the ratio of signal power to quantisation-noise power. It will be discussed in the *Noise* block.)

signal to quantisation-noise ratio

The technique is known as *non-uniform* or *non-linear encoding*, and is illustrated in Figure 5.11 for a sinusoidal signal. Note how the spacing between levels becomes progressively wider as the signal level increases. In voice telephony, 8-bit non-uniform coding is used to cover a range which would need 12 bits per sample with uniform quantisation.

non-uniform encoding
non-linear encoding

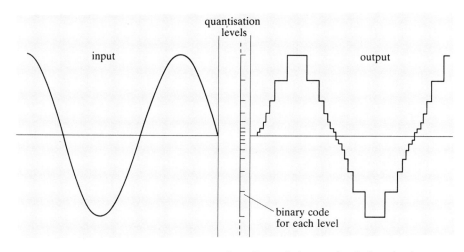

Figure 5.11 Non-uniform encoding of a sinusoid. Smaller quantisation intervals are used for small values of the signal than for large values

Such encoding – and the subsequent decoding of the received signal – is implemented electronically using a device known as a *codec* (coder/decoder). More details of codecs, and of practical non-uniform coding schemes, are given in Section 6.

codec

One of the consequences of pulse code modulation is that a single telephone channel needs a much greater bandwidth than if the speech signal were transmitted directly as an analogue signal. To quantify this, try SAQ 5.2.

SAQ 5.2 Telephone signals having bandwidth of 300 Hz to 3.4 kHz are sampled at a frequency of 8 kHz. Each sample is encoded as an 8-bit binary word and transmitted using a PCM binary signal. Compare the bandwidth required for the PCM signal with that of the original signal.

Transmission of a telephone speech signal using pulse code modulation involves approximately a ten-fold increase in bandwidth over analogue transmission, depending on the precise design of the system. Why, then, should such digital transmission be attractive economically? There are a number of reasons, but you should be able to suggest one of the most important immediately.

41

□ What is it?

■ Digital signals are inherently less susceptible to the effects of noise during transmission. This more than compensates for the introduction of quantisation distortion. Furthermore, errors that do occur can be detected and even corrected (at the expense of additional redundancy). It is often economic to accept greater bandwidth requirements in return for these advantages.

In fact, the noise and distortion suffered by an analogue signal during digital transmission can be reduced almost indefinitely by using finer quantisation, more sophisticated coding schemes, and transmission channels with greater bandwidth.

It is not only noise rejection properties that make digital transmission particularly attractive, however. By exploiting the enormous bandwidth of optical fibres, it is becoming possible to integrate all types of transmission – speech, high-quality audio, video, and data communication – within a single network using a common digital transmission technique. This has advantages for both suppliers and users of telecommunication services.

These themes are some of the most fundamental aspects of telecommunications and will all be discussed at greater length later in the course.

5.3 Signal recovery

I described earlier in this section the PAM or pulse train model of a sampled signal. A PAM signal, you should remember, is a sequence of short pulses, the heights of which represent the values of the individual samples. You should also remember that the spectrum of a properly sampled PAM signal consists of replicas of the message signal spectrum centred around multiples of the sampling frequency.

Such a PAM waveform could be physically generated at the receiver in a PCM system, using the decoded sample values to produce short pulses of appropriate height. Ideal low-pass filtering with a cut-off of half the sampling frequency would then recover the transmitted analogue signal, subject of course to quantisation noise and any errors arising during transmission.

In practice, however, signal recovery is not normally carried out in quite this way. One difficulty is that the shorter the pulses (and they need to be short for accurate signal recovery by simple low-pass filtering), the weaker the signal at the output of the filter. The most common approach in practice is to use a hold device to produce a 'staircase' waveform at the output of the decoder, rather than a pulse train, as illustrated in Figure 5.12. Subsequent ideal low-pass filtering will smooth this staircase waveform, but will *not* reconstruct the original signal without distortion: a further stage of signal processing is necessary. In this subsection I will describe this additional distortion and how it can be counteracted.

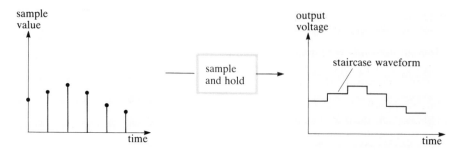

Figure 5.12 *Effect of 'holding' a sequence of sample values*

Figure 5.13 contrasts the ideal approach to signal recovery with a practical system using a hold device. In part (a) I have assumed that an ideal train of very narrow pulses is generated, and that an appropriate voltage gain is included to bring the recovered signal to the level of the original message. (Uniform scaling of the recovered signal is immaterial in practice, but it is convenient for the purpose of argument to imagine a recovered signal *identical* to the message signal apart from quantisation noise.) Part (b) of the

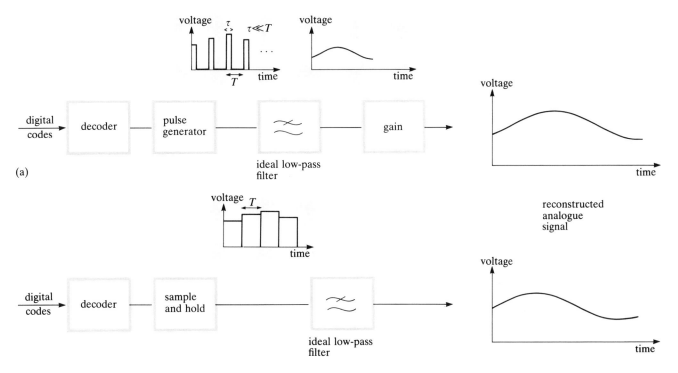

(a)

decoder → pulse generator → ideal low-pass filter → gain

digital codes →

ideal low-pass filter

digital codes → decoder → sample and hold → ideal low-pass filter →

reconstructed analogue signal

Figure 5.13 *Signal recovery from a sequence of samples: (a) by generating a train of narrow pulses; and (b) by means of a sample and hold device*

figure illustrates a practical system where a sample and hold is used to convert the PCM codes into an analogue signal – very much like a normal digital-to-analogue converter, but with the non-uniform spacing of quantisation levels described previously. The staircase waveform at the hold output can be viewed as a sequence of contiguous pulses of width T seconds. So instead of a sequence of 'very narrow' ($\tau \ll T$) pulses as in part (a) of the figure, the recovery process generates a sequence of 'full-width' pulses, and this introduces distortion.

The easiest way to quantify such distortion is in frequency domain terms, and here I shall be concerned only with amplitude distortion. By comparing the spectrum of a very short pulse with that of a 'full-width' pulse T seconds in duration, we can model the distortion introduced and then compensate by additional filtering.

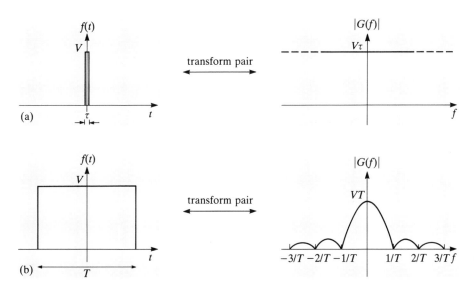

Figure 5.14 *Amplitude spectra of 'very narrow' and 'full-width' pulses*

Figure 5.14 compares the amplitude spectra of the 'very short' and 'full-width' pulses, each of height V volts. As described in Section 3, the very short pulse can be assumed to have a constant amplitude spectrum of magnitude $V\tau$, while that of the width T pulse takes the familiar form

$$VT \left| \frac{\sin (\pi Tf)}{\pi Tf} \right|$$

The ratio of these two amplitude spectra is therefore a measure of the amplitude distortion (as a function of frequency) introduced by the hold device:

$$\text{amplitude distortion} \propto \frac{\text{amplitude spectrum of long pulse}}{\text{amplitude spectrum of short pulse}}$$

$$= \frac{T}{\tau} \left| \frac{\sin (\pi T f)}{\pi T f} \right|$$

Now, the multiplier T/τ is simply a reflection of the difference in mean values of pulse trains using pulses of width τ and T. (If short pulses were generated as in Figure 5.13(a) the gain element would have to compensate by precisely this factor.) Since only the frequency dependence of the distortion is of interest, we can therefore describe the amplitude distortion by the amplitude ratio

$$|H(f)| = \left| \frac{\sin \pi T f}{\pi T f} \right|$$

In the hold recovery process of Figure 5.13(b), ideal low-pass filtering with a cut-off of half the sampling frequency $f_s/2 = 1/2T$ is assumed. Hence the distortion $|H(f)|$ is relevant only over this range, and is shown in Figure 5.15 in single-sided form. To compensate for this distortion, therefore, the ideal low-pass filter of Figure 5.13(b) needs to be replaced by a filter with an amplitude response as shown in Figure 5.16. If properly designed, such a recovery filter will compensate for the distortion introduced by the hold, and the overall recovery process will have a flat characteristic over the frequency range $0 < f < f_s/2$, as is required for the faithful reconstruction of the message signal.

In case you found this argument difficult to follow, let me recap:

1 A PAM signal consisting of very short pulses can be converted into a replica of the original analogue signal by ideal low-pass filtering.

2 Instead of generating a train of short pulses we use a hold device. The effect of the hold can be thought of as turning each short PAM pulse into a pulse of width T s.

3 To obtain a frequency domain model of the distortion introduced we compare a single, idealised PAM pulse with the corresponding rectangular pulse of width T generated by the hold.

4 The effect in the frequency domain is to turn the flat amplitude spectrum of the ideal short pulse into a $|(\sin x)/x|$ spectrum. The general frequency response model of the recovery process is therefore also of this form.

5 Ideal low-pass filtering of the PAM signal gives, in principle, perfect recovery of the message signal. Signal recovery by hold and low-pass filtering, however, needs additional compensation for the $|(\sin x)/x|$ amplitude distortion over the bandwidth of the original message signal.

A numerical example should make all this clearer. Suppose that a signal extending from dc to 4 kHz is sampled at a frequency of 8 kHz, and reconstructed using a hold followed by an ideal low-pass filter with a cut-off of 4 kHz. The gain of the system is set so that a dc component is transmitted without attenuation. By how much (in dB) would a 3 kHz component be attenuated?

In this case $T = 1/f_s = 125 \times 10^{-6}$ s. The amplitude frequency response

$$|H(f)| = \left| \frac{\sin (\pi T f)}{\pi T f} \right|$$

over the range $0 \leqslant f \leqslant f_s/2$.

Substitution of $T = 125 \times 10^{-6}$ and $f = 3 \times 10^3$ gives

$$\frac{|\sin (\pi \times 375 \times 10^{-3})|}{\pi \times 375 \times 10^{-3}} = \frac{\sin 1.178}{1.178} = 0.784$$

Expressing this amplitude ratio in decibels, with respect to the low-frequency gain of 1 gives

$$\text{amplitude ratio} = 20 \log 0.784 \, \text{dB}$$

$$= -2.1 \, \text{dB}$$

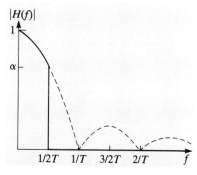

Figure 5.15 *Amplitude distortion introduced by the hold operation*

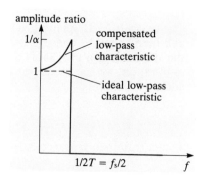

Figure 5.16 *Compensating for the amplitude distortion. Over the range $0 < f < 1/2T$ the amplitude ratio should approximate to $1/|H(f)|$, where $|H(f)|$ is as shown in Figure 5.15*

The value of the sine function is calculated using radians. Check that the value here agrees with the approximate value read from the $(\sin x)/x$ curve of Figure 3.4.

A negative value indicates attenuation. (This would often be expressed as an attenuation of 2.1 dB.)

Now try a similar example for yourself.

SAQ 5.3 As mentioned earlier, a telephone speech channel can be assumed to extend from 300 Hz to 3.4 kHz. Calculate the amplitude distortion, in dB, introduced over this range by a signal recovery process involving a hold followed by ideal low-pass filtering without additional compensation. That is, calculate the change (in dB) between the amplitude ratio at 300 Hz and at 3.4 kHz. The sampling rate is again 8 kHz.

This 2.7 dB amplitude distortion over the range of the telephone speech signal is a substantial contribution to the total permitted by CCITT standards for a PCM channel. If it were left uncorrected, then any degradation of performance due to other effects might cause the overall distortion to exceed permitted levels. Further compensation or *loss equalisation* of the type illustrated in Figure 5.16 is therefore required at the PCM decoder. The entire process of decoding a PCM signal can be represented by the block diagram of Figure 5.17, where the recovery filter has an amplitude response similar to that of Figure 5.16.

loss equalisation

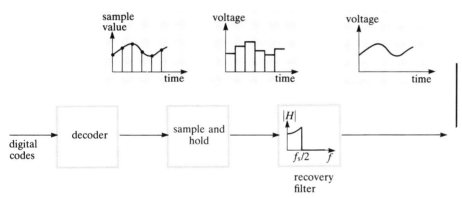

Figure 5.17 *The signal recovery process*

5.4 Summary

In pulse code modulation, samples of an analogue message signal are transmitted as digital codes. These codes are subsequently used to reconstruct the original signal at the receiver. For a baseband message signal of bandwidth B, a sampling frequency of at least $2B$ is required, although in practice sampling frequencies rather higher than the theoretical minimum are employed.

Transmitting signal samples as digital codes means that the sample values must be rounded to the nearest of a finite number of quantisation levels, thus introducing quantisation distortion. For the transmission of telephone speech signals, non-linear encoding and decoding is used, enabling a dynamic range equivalent to 12-bit uniform quantisation to be covered using 8 bits per sample. Such non-linear encoding/decoding maintains a uniform signal to quantisation-noise ratio over the full dynamic range.

Signal recovery is often performed using a sample and hold followed by low-pass filtering. The effect of the hold operation is to introduce $|(\sin x)/x|$ amplitude distortion in the recovered signal. This distortion can be counteracted by means of appropriate equalisation. Figure 5.18, which is a more detailed version of Figure 5.1, illustrates the whole process for a single PCM speech channel.

Figure 5.18 *The complete PCM process*

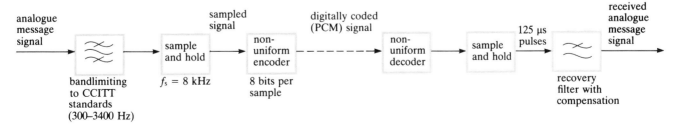

6 SYSTEMS ASPECTS OF PULSE CODE MODULATION

The previous section gave the theoretical background to the technique of pulse code modulation. I want to conclude this block by examining briefly a number of more practical aspects.

6.1 Time division multiplexing

As you saw earlier, an encoded telephone speech signal is transmitted at a rate of $64\,\text{kbits}\,\text{s}^{-1}$ (8 bits per sample; 8 kHz sampling frequency). Long-distance telephone trunks can be designed to handle data at a much greater rate than this, however. It therefore makes sense for a number of channels to share the same transmission link, using the technique of *time division multiplexing* (*TDM*). Figure 6.1 shows the basic principle, in which the multiplexing and demultiplexing are represented by rotating switches. Current practice is to use a separate encoder and decoder for each speech channel, as shown.

time division multiplexing (TDM)

Switch models like this are useful idealisations, as you saw earlier in the discussion of sampling. In practical systems, of course, such switching is performed electronically.

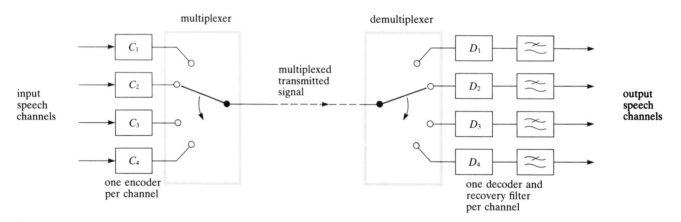

Figure 6.1 *Time division multiplexing of four speech channels*

The switch connects the transmission link to the output of each encoder in turn. Figure 6.2 illustrates how the resulting bit stream corresponds to the individual multiplexed signals for the four-channel system of Figure 6.1. The complete signal is divided into a repeating sequence of four successive time slots. When transmission begins, time slot 1 is used to transmit the 8-bit code for the first sample of channel 1; time slot 2 is then used to send the first sample of channel 2; and so on. After four time slots have elapsed the process begins again, with time slot 1 containing the code representing the *second* sample of channel 1, and so on.

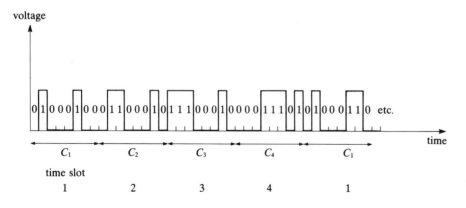

Figure 6.2 *Multiplexed bit stream for the 4-channel system of Figure 6.1*

One effect of such multiplexing is to increase the bit rate of the transmitted signal. If there are C channels, each being sampled at S samples per second, and with each sample producing an N-bit code word, the overall bit rate is

$$C \times S \times N \text{ bits s}^{-1}$$

At the receiver the multiplexed signal must be separated into the individual channels. The demultiplexer connects the incoming bit stream to each decoder for the duration of its particular time slot, thus separating the multiplexed signal into its component signals.

6.1.1 TDM hierarchies

TDM hierarchy

In practice, many more than four speech channels are multiplexed for transmission over a single link. The CCITT specifies a whole hierarchy of such multiplexing. At the lowest or *primary level*, 30 speech channels are multiplexed, together with the equivalent of two other speech channels used for the supervisory, timing and routing signals needed by the network. Thirty-two time slots are therefore needed for 30 speech channels. (This is often known as the 30 + 2 channel primary system.) Non-uniform 8-bit encoding is employed, as described earlier, with speech signals sampled at 8 kHz.

primary level

☐ What is the bit rate of the primary multiplexed signal?

■ For 32 channels, sampled 8000 times per second and encoded into 8-bit words, the overall bit rate is

$$32 \times 8000 \times 8 = 2.048 \times 10^6 \text{ bits s}^{-1}$$

This rate is usually expressed as 2.048 Mbits s^{-1}.

The time slots are numbered from 0 to 31. Time slots 1 to 15 and 17 to 31 are used for the 30 speech channels, leaving slots 0 and 16 for the control information, referred to earlier. The composite digital signal of time slots 0 to 31 is referred to as a *frame*.

frame

☐ How many bits are there in a frame in this system?

■ $8 \times 32 = 256$ bits.

A complete frame is shown schematically in Figure 6.3.

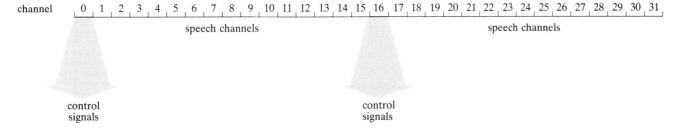

Even a bit rate of 2.048 Mbits s^{-1} does not use the national and international telephone networks efficiently, since microwave, satellite and optical fibre links have bandwidths much greater than needed for such a data rate. The primary multiplexed signals are therefore themselves multiplexed in groups of four to form successively higher levels of a *hierarchy*. This is illustrated in Figure 6.4. You may notice that bit rates at the higher levels of the hierarchy are not exact multiples of 2.048 Mbits s^{-1}. This is to enable the overall system to multiplex lower levels which are not quite synchronised, and also to provide time slots for control information for tasks such as maintaining higher-level synchronisation of individual primary level frames.

hierarchy

Figure 6.4 *CCITT digital TDM hierarchy*

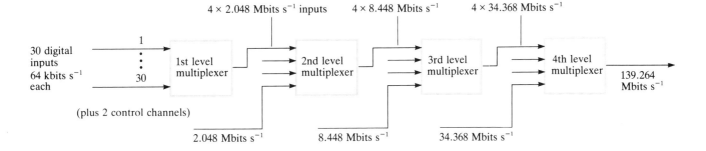

Figure 6.4 illustrates the most recent CCITT hierarchy at the time of writing (1988). However, systems within individual countries are already operating at bit rates in excess of the nominal 140 Mbits s^{-1} of the highest level: for example, British Telecom currently operates a number of optical fibre links at a nominal 565 Mbits s^{-1} and even higher rates will shortly be introduced. (The most recent CCITT recommendations note the use of levels corresponding to four multiplexed 140 Mbits s^{-1}, but this level has not yet been standardised.)

6.2 Regenerative repeaters

The effects of noise and distortion introduced during the transmission of any signal accumulate as the length of the transmission path increases. This is true for signals transmitted by copper wire, optical fibre, radio or any other means: there is always a limit beyond which the degradation becomes unacceptable. In the transmission of analogue telephone signals via copper cable, repeater amplifiers or loading coils were spaced at regular intervals throughout the link, in an attempt to minimise the effect of noise and distortion. A similar strategy has to be adopted with digital transmission, although there are two important differences.

You should remember from earlier sections of this block that it is not important for a digital signal to be received exactly as transmitted. As long as it is still possible to make correct decisions about signal states, then a perfect copy of the original digital signal can be produced by appropriate threshold detection, assuming accurate retiming is possible. In a digital system, therefore, error rates can be kept very low indeed by carrying out such *regeneration* of the original signal at intervals along the link. This procedure is quite different from the use of repeater amplifiers in an analogue system, and is best thought of as a combination of a digital receiver and transmitter in a single unit known as a *regenerative repeater*. The general idea is illustrated in Figure 6.5. The major restriction on spacing is that the input to the receiver module of an intermediate repeater should not suffer so much from noise and distortion that the transmitted digital signal cannot be reconstructed. It is therefore usual to design PCM systems with sufficiently small spacing between repeaters to ensure that the probability of errors occurring is very small. It may seem from this description that there is no limit to the length of the complete link: in principle, an arbitrarily high number of regenerators could be used. In practice, however, even regeneration introduces *some* degradation. One major difficulty is that the strict timing of the digital signal suffers from repeated regeneration, and this ultimately leads to decision errors. The phenomenon is known as *jitter*, and it is an important practical problem in digital transmission.

regeneration

regenerative repeater

jitter

The second important difference between regenerators and repeaters concerns the spacing. In early PCM telephony, when the digital signals were transmitted using cables originally designed for analogue transmission, regenerators were inserted every 1800 m. This was mainly because access was already provided at this interval for inserting the inductors needed to give

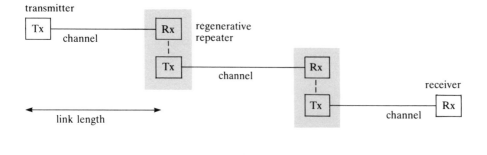

Figure 6.5 Splitting a long link into a number of short links with intermediate regeneration

48

cables the frequency characteristics necessary for adequate analogue performance. At the time of writing (1988), however, optical fibre cables 100 km or so in length can be used for digital transmission without regeneration. For a relatively small country such as the UK, therefore, the importance of regeneration outside exchanges seems to be declining, although it will remain a vital feature of transcontinental or submarine cables.

6.3 Codecs

Codecs were briefly mentioned in Section 5.2. A codec can be implemented as a single integrated circuit which carries out sampling, quantisation, and coding of a transmitted signal, as well as decoding and recovery of a received signal. Codecs are widely used within telephone exchange equipment, and will be found increasingly in telephone terminals themselves as digital links are extended as far as the end user. A simplified block diagram of a codec is given in Figure 6.6.

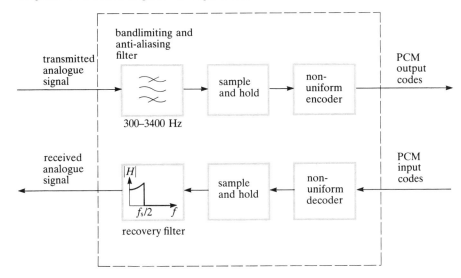

Figure 6.6 *Simplified block diagram of a codec*

The band-pass filter on the analogue input side limits the speech signal to a frequency range of 300–3400 Hz, with the precise details of attenuation over the stop bands and pass band being closely specified by CCITT recommendations. This filter also acts as an anti-aliasing filter by effectively removing speech components above 4 kHz, half the sampling frequency.

Two different non-linear encoding/decoding characteristics are specified by the CCITT, known as *μ-law* and *A-law*. Both characteristics are similar in form to the curve of Figure 6.7, although the precise mathematical function differs in the two cases. In the figure, the V-axis from -1 to $+1$ represents the full range of input voltages. The digital codes are imagined as equally spaced along the y-axis, so that the range of input voltages represented by the codes in interval A near the origin is much smaller than that represented by an equal interval B near the maximum, as described in Section 5.2. The terms A-law and $μ$-law are derived from the mathematical expressions for the precise characteristic used. The digital codes used for the 256 quantisation levels in the two schemes are listed in full in CCITT recommendations, and commercial codecs are available in both $μ$-law and A-law versions. European telephone systems use A-law, and North American and Japanese systems $μ$-law.

Figure 6.8 gives details of the 8-bit, A-law encoder/decoder characteristic used in European PCM systems. The complete input range $-V$ to $+V$ volts is broken into 13 linear segments as shown. (The first positive and negative segments form a single straight line.) The levels are referred to as 0 to 127 positive and 0 to 127 negative. The most significant bit of a digital code is 1 for a positive sample and 0 for a negative sample. In the figure, the symbol XXXX in a code means that those particular bits vary from 0000 to 1111 from the lowest to the highest decision level in the particular segment. Segment 1 is twice as wide as the others, using 32 rather than 16 codes.

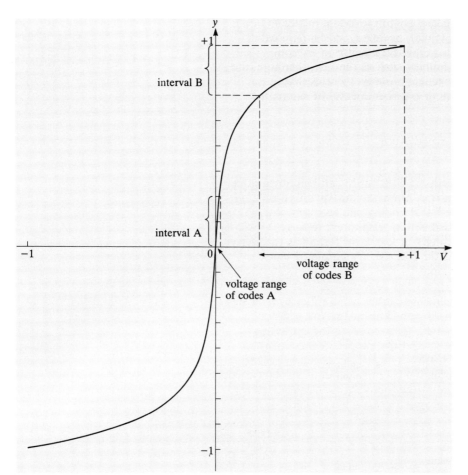

For A-law:

$$y = \frac{1 + \ln(AV)}{1 + \ln A}, \quad 1/A \leqslant |V| \leqslant 1$$

$$y = \frac{AV}{1 + \ln A}, \quad 0 \leqslant |V| \leqslant 1/A$$

where A is a constant.

For μ-law:

$$y = \frac{\ln(1 + \mu V)}{1 + \mu}, \quad 0 \leqslant |V| \leqslant 1$$

where μ is a constant.

Figure 6.7 *Non-uniform encoder characteristic. (The mathematical expressions defining μ-law and A-law are for information only, and will not be assessed)*

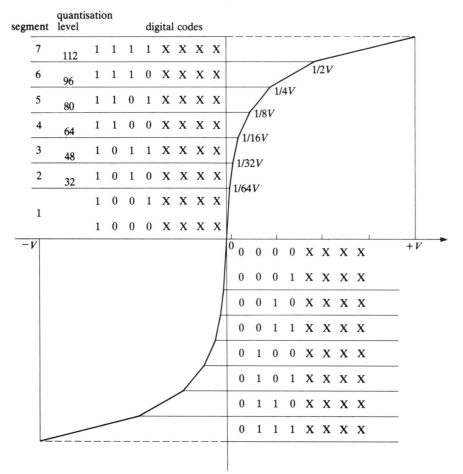

Figure 6.8 *Coding scheme for CCITT European A-law PCM*

As mentioned in Section 3, if the smallest quantisation interval of Figure 6.8 were used over the entire range, 12 bits per sample would be required. The effect of the non-linear coding may therefore be thought of as 'compressing' a 12-bit to an 8-bit representation. Similarly, the non-linear decoding process 'expands' the codes again to the full dynamic range. For this reason the complete, non-linear, encoding/decoding process is often known as *companding* (compressing/expanding).

companding

☐ What is the range of binary codes used for (i) positive segment 1 and (ii) negative segment 4?

■ From the figure, the lowest code in positive segment 1 is 10000000, while the highest is 10011111. Similarly negative segment 4 uses codes from 01000000 to 01001111.

The CCITT-recommended μ-law is broadly similar to the A-law, although the way digital codes are allocated to the various quantisation levels is different. (For example, the lowest natural binary codes are allocated to the largest negative quantization levels.) Full details are given in CCITT (1985).

I should now like you to read the following extract from a Plessey data sheet for a codec. Unless you have specialised prior knowledge you will not understand all the details given. However, by comparing the extract with Figure 6.6 you should be able to understand the important functional characteristics of the device described. I have underlined a number of important terms, all of which have been discussed in detail in this block. Please read the extract, and then attempt the following SAQs, illustrating your answers with sketches where appropriate.

MV3506/3507/3507A

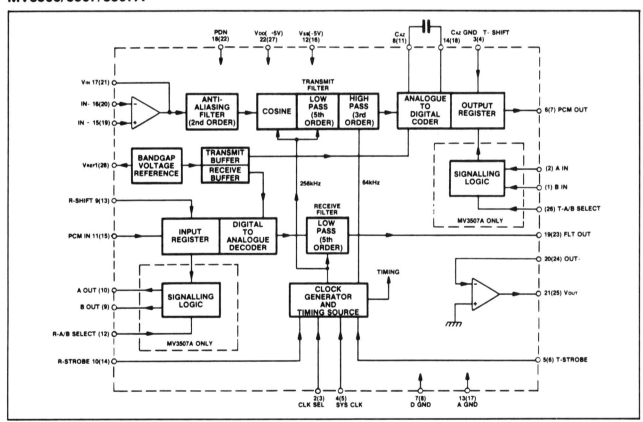

MV3506 A-Law codec with filter
MV3507 μ-Law codec with filter
The MV3506 and MV3507 are silicon gate CMOS Companding Encoder/Decoder integrated circuits designed to implement the per channel voice frequency Codecs used in PCM systems. The chips contain the band-limiting filters and the analogue to digital conversion circuits that conform to the desired transfer characteristic. The MV3506 provides the European A-law companding and the MV3507 provides the North American μ-Law companding characteristic. [...]

Transmit section

Input analogue signals first enter the chip at the uncommitted op. amp terminals. This op. amp allows gain trim to be used to set 0TLP in the system. From the V$_{IN}$ pin the signal enters the 2nd Order analogue anti-aliasing filter. This filter eliminates the need for any off-chip filtering as it provides attenuation of 34 dB (typ) at 256 kHz and 44 dB (typ) at 512 kHz. From the cosine filter the signal enters a 5th Order low-pass filter clocked at 256 kHz, followed by a 3rd Order high-pass filter clocked at 64 kHz. The resulting band-pass characteristics meet the CCITT G.711, G.712 and G.733 specifications. Some representative attenuations are 26 dB (typ) from 0 to 60 Hz and 35 dB (typ) from 4.6 kHz to 100 kHz. The output of the high-pass filter is sampled by a capacitor array at the sampling rate of 8 kHz. [...]

Included in the circuitry of the MV3507 is 'All Zero' code suppression so that negative input signal values between decision values numbers 127 and 128 are encoded as 00000010. This prevents loss of repeater synchronisation by T1 line clock recovery circuitry as there are never more than 15 consecutive zeroes. [...]

The MV3507 is the μ-law code that uses the lowest natural binary codes for the largest negative quantisation levels.

Receive section

A receive shift clock, variable between the frequencies of 64 kHz to 2.048 MHz, clocks the PCM data into the input buffer register once every sampling period. A charge proportional to the received PCM data word appears on the decoder capacitor array. A sample and hold initialised to zero by a narrow pulse at the beginning of each sampling period integrates the charge and holds for the rest of the sampling period. A switched-capacitor 5th Order low-pass filter clocked at 256 kHz smooths the sampled and held signal. It also performs the loss equalisation to compensate for the $\sin x/x$ distortion due to the sample and hold operation.

(Courtesy of Austria Mikro Systeme International Ltd)

SAQ 6.1 Explain what is meant by aliasing, and how it can be prevented. Why is a sampling rate of 8 kHz suitable for the digital transmission of telephone speech signals?

SAQ 6.2 What is meant by 'clock recovery', and why should the transmission of more than 15 consecutive 0s affect this.

SAQ 6.3 Explain why the receive section of the codec includes a low-pass filter. What is 'loss equalisation', and why in this case does it need to compensate for '$(\sin x)/x$ distortion'?

6.4 Summary

Time division multiplexing allows many independent speech channels to be transmitted over a single link. CCITT recommendations specify a four-level TDM hierarchy for the international PCM system.

Very long links can be split into shorter sections, with regeneration of the digital signal at intermediate stages. The spacing of regenerative repeaters depends on the transmission medium, but can be up to 100 km for optical fibre links.

In practice, the entire process of sampling and encoding the speech signal, and decoding and recovering the received PCM signal, can be carried out by a single integrated circuit known as a codec. Codecs are available in μ-law and A-law versions, depending on the encoding/decoding characteristic used.

7 BLOCK SUMMARY

In this block a number of standard, idealised signal models have been developed and applied to digital telecommunication systems. Section 2 looked at the representation of periodic signals as a line spectrum, and used the spectrum of a 'worst-case' digital signal to illustrate a fundamental rule of digital communications: the maximum theoretical signalling rate over a bandlimited channel of bandwidth B Hz is $2B$ states s^{-1}.

In Section 3, standard frequency domain models of individual data pulses were developed, and it was shown that such isolated pulses have continuous, rather than line spectra. The spectra of various idealised pulses were described; particularly important are the rectangular pulse with the $(\sin x)/x$ spectrum, and the pulse with the raised-cosine spectrum. The properties of these spectra were used in Section 4 to analyse intersymbol interference (ISI), and it was shown that there is a trade-off between immunity to ISI and channel bandwidth. Shaping data pulses can reduce ISI, but only at the cost of additional bandwidth: the raised cosine spectrum was shown to have particularly desirable properties in this respect.

Digital signals for transmission over the public switched network must also possess other desirable properties, such as a zero dc component and sufficient timing information to maintain synchronisation. The elementary properties of codes to ensure this were also discussed in Section 4.

Sections 5 and 6 introduced the theoretical basis of pulse code modulation together with some systems aspects. The spectral models of Sections 2 and 3 were extended to include sampled signals, which possess periodic spectra, and the consequences of this for the choice of sampling rate and for signal recovery were described. The sampling theorem states that a continuous signal of bandwidth B must be sampled at a frequency of at least $2B$ in order to prevent loss of information. In practice, sampling rates rather higher than the theoretical minimum are used. In Section 6 the CCITT PCM multiplexing hierarchy was outlined and the need for regeneration of digital signals during long-distance transmission was explained. Finally, a codec was presented in terms of its functional components.

REFERENCES AND FURTHER READING

CCITT (1985) *Digital Networks/Transmission Systems and Multiplexing Equipment*, Red Book Vol. III, Fascicle III.3, Recommendations G.700–G.956, CCITT.

The CCITT recommendations are a good source of detailed practical information relating to Sections 5 and 6 of this block. The recommendations above relate to PCM and digital multiplexing.

LYNN, P.A. (1982) *An Introduction to the Analysis and Processing of Signals*, 2nd ed., Macmillan.

LYNN, P.A. (1986) *Electronic Signals and Systems*, Macmillan.

These two books are recommended if you wish to learn more about signal analysis and processing. The second one covers the subject at an elementary level (first- or second-year undergraduate), while the first book covers more material at a faster pace.

OPEN UNIVERSITY (1984) T326 *Electronic Signal Processing*, The Open University Press.

PEEBLES, P.Z. JNR (1987) *Digital Communication Systems*, Prentice–Hall.

SCHWARTZ, M. (1980) *Information, Transmission, Modulation and Noise*, 3rd ed., McGraw–Hill.

A classic text with a wide coverage. Both Peebles and Schwartz include material similar to Sections 3–5 of this block but at a more advanced level; they also cover topics relevant to other parts of T322.

SHANNON, C.E. (1948) A mathematical theory of communication, *Bell Systems Technical Journal*, Vol. 27, pp. 379–423.

SAQ 2.1   A frequency of 8 kHz is twice the 4 kHz cut-off of the filter. Figure 2.6 shows that for a first-order low-pass filter the amplitude ratio and phase shift at $2 f_c$ are about -7 dB and $-63°$ respectively. Hence if the transmitted amplitude is 10 V, the received amplitude V_r is given by

$$-7 = 20 \log \frac{V_r}{10}$$

$$-0.35 = \log \frac{V_r}{10}$$

Taking antilogs of each side gives

$$0.45 = \frac{V_r}{10} \quad \text{(2 significant figures)}$$

Hence the received sinusoid has an amplitude of 4.5 V and a phase lag of 63°.

SAQ 2.2   The line spectrum will be similar to Figure 2.9 except that the repetition period $T_p = 4T$ rather than $2T$. Hence the first harmonic has a frequency $f_1 = 1/T_p = 1/4T$; the third harmonic $f_3 = 3/4T$; and so on. The spectrum is drawn in Figure A.1. (Note that the scaling of the waveform time axis by a factor of 2 with respect to Figure 2.7 results in a corresponding scaling of the frequency axis by $\frac{1}{2}$ in comparison with Figure 2.9.)

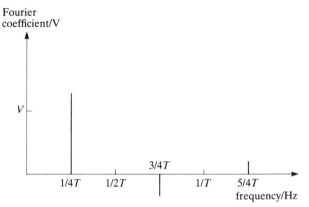

Figure A.1   *Answer to SAQ 2.2*

SAQ 2.3   If the duration of a signalling element is T, then the first harmonic of Figure 2.8 will occur at $f_1 = 1/2T$. Here $T = 10^{-2}$, so $f_1 = 1/(2 \times 10^{-2}) = 50$ Hz.

(a)   Figure 2.6 shows that a first-order low-pass filter with cut-off of 150 Hz will pass a 50 Hz component ($f_c/3$) with virtually no attenuation (but note the phase lag of about 20°). The third harmonic at 150 Hz will be attenuated by 3 dB, however, and higher harmonics by correspondingly more. We should therefore expect appreciable distortion of the original waveform.

(b)   For a filter with cut-off of 1.5 kHz, all significant components of the square wave will be passed with amplitude and phase relationships only slightly modified. The waveform will therefore suffer only slight distortion.

Alternatively, you may be familiar with the expression for the step response 10% to 90% rise time

$$t_r \times B = 0.35$$

where B is the filter bandwidth. Taking the cut-off frequencies as the channel bandwidths gives

$$t_r \simeq 2 \text{ ms for } B = 150 \text{ Hz}$$
$$t_r \simeq 0.2 \text{ ms for } B = 1.5 \text{ kHz}$$

These rise times lead to the same conclusion, since a rise time of 2 ms is highly significant for a 10 ms pulse, while 0.2 ms is much less so. Note, however, that the rise time expression applies only to *step* changes, whereas the frequency response approach is general, given some knowledge of the input spectrum.

SAQ 2.4

(a)   With binary transmission the signalling rate is 4800 baud. Hence:

$$4800 = 2 \times B$$

and the minimum theoretical bandwidth is:

$$B = 2.4 \text{ kHz}.$$

(b)   With quaternary transmission the signalling rate is 2400 baud. Hence the minimum theoretical bandwidth is half the value in (a) at 1.2 kHz.

SAQ 2.5   The spectrum of Figure 2.12 is identical to Figure 2.9 apart from a zero-frequency line of magnitude V. The time domain waveform is therefore identical to Figure 2.7, but raised by V volts, as shown in Figure A.2.

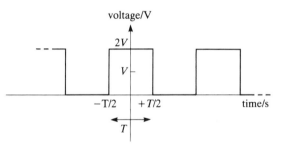

Figure A.2   *Square wave with dc component (mean value) of V volts*

SAQ 2.6

(a) See Figure A.3.

In all cases note that the double-sided amplitudes are half the corresponding single-sided ones; and the phase spectra are antisymmetric about $\omega = 0$.

(b) See Figure A.4. Note that the dc line is the same height in both single-sided and double-sided representations.

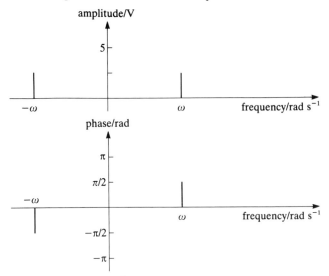

(i) $f(t) = 5 \cos (\omega t + \pi/2)$

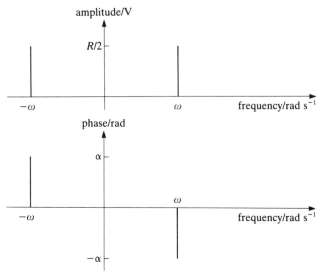

(ii) $f(t) = R \cos (\omega t - \alpha)$

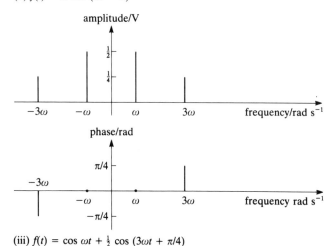

(iii) $f(t) = \cos \omega t + \frac{1}{2} \cos (3\omega t + \pi/4)$

Figure A.3 *Answer to SAQ 2.6(a)*

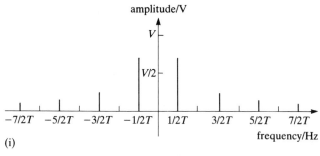

(i)

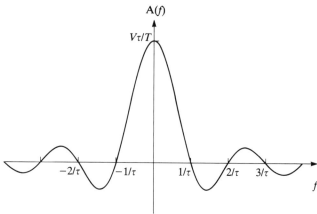

(ii)

Figure A.4 *Bilateral amplitude spectra of square waves (i) without and (ii) with a dc component*

SAQ 3.1 See Figure A.5. The zero crossings of $(\sin x)/x$ occur at integral multiples of π. Hence the zero crossings of $[\sin (\pi\tau f)]/\pi\tau f$ occur at frequencies which are integral multiples of $1/\tau$ as required. For $f = m/T$ the expression $A(f)$ is equivalent to a_m.

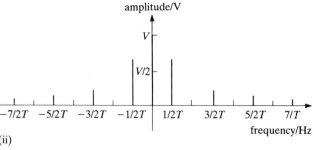

Figure A.5 *Answer to SAQ 3.1*

SAQ 3.2   See Figure A.6. In each case $G(0) = V\tau$, and the first zero crossing takes place at $1/\tau$ Hz.

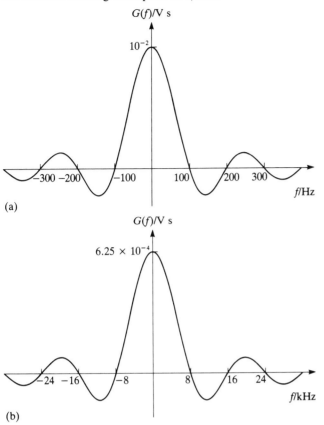

Figure A.6   *Answer to SAQ 3.2*

SAQ 3.3

(a)   For a pulse width τ seconds, the first zero crossing in the spectrum takes place at $1/\tau$ Hz. Hence $1/\tau = 500\,\text{Hz}$ and $\tau = 1/500\,\text{s} \equiv 2\,\text{ms}$. $V\tau = 10^{-3}\,\text{V s}$, so

$$V \times 2 \times 10^{-3} = 10^{-3}$$

and

$$V = 0.5\,\text{V}.$$

(b)   Similarly, we have $\tau = 1/20 = 0.05\,\text{s}$ and $V\tau = 0.5\,\text{V s}$. Hence

$$V = 10\,\text{V}.$$

The pulses are sketched in Figure A.7. (Remember that the pulses are drawn from $-\tau/2$ to $+\tau/2$.)

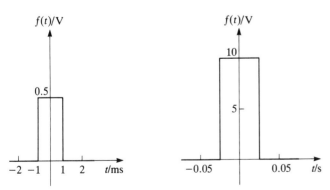

Figure A.7   *Answer to SAQ 3.3*

SAQ 3.4

(a)   The two pulses are similar in shape, with a factor of 5 difference in duration. The spectra will therefore also be similar, but scaled in frequency by a factor of $1/5$. The spectra are sketched in Figure A.8(a), which shows precisely what I mean by such scaling. Note the difference in height of the spectra as a result of the difference in pulse *area*. Note also the zero values: Figure 3.13 gave the spectrum of a pulse width 2τ, not τ.

(b)   The two pulses are of the same area and width. As was noted earlier, the high-frequency side lobes will be much more pronounced in the rectangular pulse spectrum than in that of the triangular pulse. Reference to Figure 3.13 allows the amplitude spectra to be sketched as shown in Figure A.8(b). Note again the zero values in the spectra of the two pulses.

(c)   The two pulses are of similar height, area, and duration, but the rectangular pulse has sharp discontinuities, while the other is similar to the raised cosine pulse of Figure 3.13 in that it exhibits smooth changes in both voltage level and slope. The rectangular pulse has the familiar $(\sin x)/x$ spectrum. In the absence of precise information about the shape of the second pulse an accurate spectrum cannot be drawn, but it is reasonable to expect that the side lobes in the spectrum will have about $1/T$ spacing, and that the amplitudes of these side lobes will decrease with increasing frequency much faster than those of the $(\sin x)/x$ spectrum.

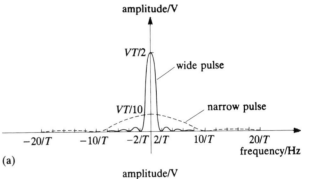

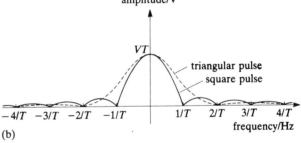

Figure A.8   *Answer to SAQ 3.4*

SAQ 4.1   Both worst cases correspond to the waveform shown in Figure A.9: a squarewave with period $2T$, where T is the duration of one signalling element. As seen earlier in Section 3, the first harmonic of such a waveform occurs at $1/2T$ and there is a null in the spectrum at $1/T$, the data rate. Neither line spectrum contains a data rate component. (Refer to Figure 2.8 or 2.9 if necessary.)

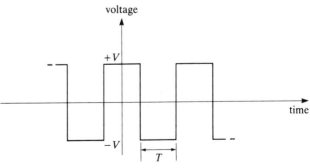

Figure A.9   *Worst-case waveform for both zero-mean bipolar signal and AMI signal*

SAQ 4.2 A long sequence of binary 0s corresponding to a steady zero voltage.

SAQ 5.1 The spectrum of the sampled signal consists of repeated versions of Figure 5.6(b) centred around multiples of 100 Hz, the sampling frequency. The required section of the spectrum is shown in Figure A.10.

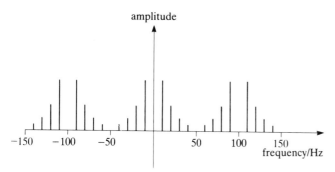

Figure A.10 *Repeated amplitude line spectrum of a sampled, bandlimited, periodic signal*

SAQ 5.2 A rate of 8000 samples per second, each coded using 8 bits, means a data rate of 64 kbits s^{-1}. The theoretical minimum bandwidth using a binary signal is therefore 32 kHz. This is around ten times the bandwidth of the original signal. In practice, an even greater bandwidth would be required. For example, using raised cosine pulse shaping means a doubling of the theoretical minimum to 64 kHz.

SAQ 5.3

Given $|H(f)| = \left| \dfrac{\sin \pi Tf}{\pi Tf} \right|$

where $T = 125 \times 10^{-6}$ s, we need to calculate $|H(300)|/|H(3400)| = A$, say.

Hence $A = \dfrac{|\sin \pi T300|}{|\sin \pi T3400|} \dfrac{\pi\cancel{T}3400}{\pi\cancel{T}300}$

(Note that I have simplified the expression before substituting for T.)

$$A = \frac{34}{3} \frac{|\sin (3.75 \times \pi \times 10^{-2})|}{|\sin (4.25 \times \pi \times 10^{-1})|}$$

$$= \frac{34}{3} \left[\frac{0.1175}{0.9724} \right]$$

$$= 1.37 \text{ (3 significant figures)}$$

Converting to decibels we have

$$A = \frac{|H(300)|}{|H(3400)|} = 20 \log 1.37 \text{ dB}$$

$$= 2.7 \text{ dB (2 significant figures)}$$

The positive value of dB indicates that the amplitude ratio is greater at 300 Hz than at 3400 Hz. If $|H(3400)/H(300)|$ had been calculated, then the result would have been -2.7 dB, indicating attenuation at 3400 Hz with respect to 300 Hz.

SAQ 6.1 Aliasing is the phenomenon in which a high-frequency signal component is misinterpreted as a lower-frequency one, owing to the use of a sampling rate of less than twice the frequency of the high-frequency component. (In an assignment a sketch like Figure 5.2 or Figure 5.8 should be included here.)

To prevent aliasing, the analogue signal should be strictly bandlimited before sampling in accordance with the sampling theorem. Anti-aliasing filters are used to ensure this by removing all components above a given frequency. (Note that the second-order anti-aliasing filter mentioned in the data sheet is present because of the higher-rate sampling used by the digital filters in the codec. Band limiting of the telephone speech signals is carried out by the 'transmit filter' to CCITT standards.)

The spectrum of a typical telephone speech signal extends up to 3.4 kHz. The minimum sampling rate according to the sampling theorem is therefore 6.8 kHz. A practical system uses a sampling rate higher than this minimum in order to ease demands on the filters used for signal recovery. (No practical filter can possess a perfectly sharp cut-off.) A sampling frequency of 8 kHz is a suitable compromise, allowing a sufficient margin for recovery filters to be realised.

SAQ 6.2 Clock recovery is one term for the extraction of a timing signal from the digital waveform. In order to extract a suitable timing signal there must be sufficiently frequent transitions between signalling states. Hence, unless appropriate action is taken, a long run of 0s, represented by a steady 0 V digital signal, can result in the loss of synchronisation.

As was noted in Section 4, line codes have been designed to overcome this problem, but in its μ-law version the codec itself includes some rudimentary protection against such loss of synchronisation. If the 'all zero' code is suppressed, then the worst-case run of 0s would actually be 10000000 followed by 00000001, that is, 14 consecutive 0s. (CCITT μ-law recommendations allow a maximum of 15 consecutive 0s, so the codec actually does slightly better than the standard allows.)

SAQ 6.3 The spectrum of a sampled signal (represented by very narrow pulses) includes high-frequency replicas of the original message signal, as was illustrated in Figure 5.5. Signal recovery therefore involves low-pass filtering to remove high-frequency components.

In this case, a sample-and-hold device forms part of the recovery process. This introduces amplitude distortion of the form

$$|H(f)| = \frac{|\sin \pi Tf|}{|\pi Tf|}$$

where T is the duration of one signalling element, in comparison with the ideal spectrum. Loss equalisation is the process of correcting this amplitude distortion by means of a special filter circuit. In this particular case, the equalising filter is combined with the low-pass filter as a single, 5th order recovery filter circuit.

Acknowledgements

Grateful acknowledgement is made to the following sources for permission to use material in this block:

Text
Text on p. 52 is reproduced courtesy of Austria Mikro Systeme International Ltd.

Figures
Figure 2.1: O'Reilly, J. J. *Telecommunication Principles*, 1984, Van Nostrand Reinhold (UK); *Figure 6.8*: Freeman, R. L. *Telecommunication Transmission Handbook*, © 1981, John Wiley & Sons, Inc.; *Figure 6.9*: Austria Mikro Systeme International Ltd.

T322
Digital Telecommunications